Max OUT
I Want It All

Zenovia Andrews

Copyright © 2013 Zenovia Andrews

First Edition

All rights reserved.

No part of this publication may be reproduced, stored in a retrieval system or transmitted in any form or by any means, electronic, mechanical, photocopying, recording, scanning or otherwise, except under the terms of the Copyright, Designs and Patents Act 1988 or under the terms of a license issued by the Copyright Licensing Agency Ltd.

ISBN-13: 978-0-9888584-0-4
Book Cover & Design by PIXEL eMarketing INC.

Legal Disclaimer

The Publisher and the Authors make no representations or warranties with respect to the accuracy or completeness of the contents of this work and specifically disclaim all warranties, including without limitation warranties of fitness for a particular purpose. No warranty maybe created or extended by sales or promotional materials. The advice and strategies contained herein may not be suitable for every situation.

Neither the publishers nor the authors shall be liable for damages arising herefrom. The fact that an organization or website is referred to in this work as a citation and/or a potential source of further information does not mean that the author or the publisher endorses the information the organization or website it may provide or recommendations it may make.

Further, readers should be aware that Internet websites listed in this work may have changed or disappeared between when this work was written and when it is read.

★ *To protect the privacy of my clients some identity information has been changed when quoting success stories and case studies.*

Dedication

This book is dedicated with everlasting love to my husband, Anthony Andrews II. I can't imagine this journey in life without you by my side. You are the wind beneath my wings!

"Husbands, love your wives, just as Christ loved the church and gave himself up for her."
—Ephesians 5:25

Acknowledgments

To my *Lord and Savior*: Thank you for your unmerited favor. I can't even begin to imagine where I would be without your grace.

To my amazing husband of 16 years, *Anthony Andrews II*, for his devotion, patience, and support in this legacy work, and...

To my loving children, *Anovia and Anthony Andrews*, for giving mommy "quiet time" to work on this project.

To my entire family: Thank you for always supporting me and encouraging me to "Dominate My Gift Zone."

Contents

Introduction: Living Life to the Max 1

Chapter 1. The Don't Quit Mantra. 3
   Quitting and Failure 4
   Leading a "Don't Quit" Lifestyle 5
   Five Ways to Overcome Anything.. 7
   Poetry and Emotion... 9
   Your Dreams and Quitting................................. 11
   Fulfillment through Perseverance 12

Chapter 2. Work It to Win It 15
   Your Life Under a Microscope... 16
   Decision Making and Success... 17
   Working on Yourself... 19
   Working on Your Career and Happiness 20
   Working on Your Family 22
   Working on Your Spiritual Wellbeing 24

Chapter 3. Got Game? Know Who You Are! 27
   What Are Your Unique Talents? 28
   How to Use These Talents for Success 29
   Empowering Yourself 31
   Getting Game If You Need Some 32
   10 Questions to Help You Understand Yourself 34
   Planning for Strengths and Weaknesses............................. 35

Chapter 4. Embrace the Transformation Process . . 39
   The Power of Positive Thinking... 40

How Positive Thinking Can Transform Your Life 41
Becoming Who You Are 43
10 Positive Thinking Mantras 44
Mistakes Are Learning Opportunities 46
Transform and MaxOut! 48

Chapter 5. Courage in Your Career 51
Where Your Career Is Right Now 52
Where Your Heart Lies 53
The Courage to Work to Win 55
Taking Leaps of Faith 56
Faith for Motivation and Success 58
Daring to Dream 59

**Chapter 6. Getting Held Back and
Breaking Forward 63**
The Obstacles in Life 64
Drained of Your Potential 65
Identifying What Empowers and Drains You 67
Breaking Free of Your Bonds 68
God's Plan for You 70
Following Your Desired Path 71

Chapter 7. Understanding and Destroying Fear. . . 75
What Fear Does to Your Life 76
Fear and Potential 77
The Art of Overcoming Fear 79
The Real Meaning of MaxOut 81
Keeping Fear at Bay 82
Courage, Faith, and Strength 84

Chapter 8. Living the "I Want It All" Life 87

What's Wrong with Wanting It All? 88
Carpe Diem: Seize the Day 89
Procrastination and Potential 91
Listing Your Heart's Desires 92
How to Get From Want to Have 94
Positive Reinforcement 96

Chapter 9. How To Max Out Your Potential 99
Turning Potential into Reality 100
The Scarier Reality 101
MaxOut to Win It All 103
Living by Example 104
Inspiration and Motivation to MaxOut 106
Your Life, Your Rules 108

Chapter 10. Six Lessons in Personal Growth 111
#1: The Positive Approach 112
#2: Attacking the Problem 113
#3: Moving Forward All the Time 115
#4: Never Give Up 117
#5: Knowing Your Limits Are Few 118
#6: Getting the Most from Life 120

Conclusion 123

References 125

About the Author 137

Introduction: Living Life to the Max

Right now you're living life on auto-pilot. You may not even realize what this means or how significantly it impacts where you are—but it does. The thoughts that run through your mind each day dictate your attitude, and it's this attitude that leads you down the paths you've walked in your life.

Though it may not feel that way, you are where you are because you've chosen to live with an attitude that doesn't embrace life in all its glory. Systematically, you've realized that concepts like "success," "happiness," and "fulfillment" are abstract and increasingly difficult to experience because of the choices you've made.

What if I told you I could teach you how to change all that? For the last fifteen years I've been working with people and helping them fulfill their destinies by showing them how to live life to the max every single day.

Inside you is a light that you were born with. We were all born with it, though only a few choose to focus and use this light in our lives. Some call it potential, others destiny. For many, as the years roll by, the light gets dimmer—as attitudes fail. You convince yourself that you are unable to achieve success and live a life without it.

You should never settle for an unsuccessful life! You have no idea how incredible your life can be if you adjust your attitude and max out your potential. It's only when I began to do this that my life turned around. Progressively over the years, I've seen hundreds of others do the same thing, and it's changed their lives.

Your attitude determines your altitude. It's an old saying but one that rings true even now.

Somewhere along the way we choose to be average because we give up on ourselves. This book is about rejecting how your life is right now. You deserve better! There's NO reason why you shouldn't be the person you've always wanted to be.

It begins with a leap of faith and ends in your ultimate potential being released in this world. God has given you your own special abilities. While society tries to crush them out of you, we never lose that intense feeling that we should be doing something else or achieving more. I have it, you have it—but so few people listen and seek happiness.

I never could have gotten to where I am now without a positive attitude. Too many things tried to hold me back and make me a non-believer in my potential. Luckily, I'm persistent and forced myself through those many obstacles that life threw in my path.

You too can learn to overcome ANY obstacle—no matter how difficult—if you believe in your potential. Stop living life on auto-pilot and let's start maxing out your potential!

[01]

The Don't Quit Mantra

"I hated every minute of training, but I said, 'Don't quit. Suffer now and live the rest of your life as a champion."

MUHAMMAD ALI

One of the key lessons I've learnt during my journey as a life coach is that the most powerful intangible drive in our lives is our will. The strength of your will dictates how motivated you are in life as well as in the things that you do daily.

Having the will to never give up is a habit you can learn. Life teaches us to give up and move on—to be more comfortable. The irony is that we end up settling, and we are never really comfortable again. You need to seek out the truth, and today that truth is about quitting.

Quitting and Failure

I learned everything I needed to know about quitting from my birth parents, who abandoned me when I was six months old. It took me a long time to understand it, but they must have been terrified of their potential future with me in order to give me up like that.

As a society, we're taught that when the going gets tough, the tough get going. It's easier to abandon our responsibilities than think for even a moment that we can handle them. We like to hide or pass the buck, and we are so unwilling to test ourselves when things get hard. By the time we are teenagers, we are all experts in the art of quitting and failure.

Philippians 4:12–13 says, *"I know how to be brought low, and I know how to abound. In any and every circumstance, I have learned the secret of facing plenty and hunger, abundance and need. I can do all things through him who strengthens me."*

What if I told you that changing your attitude would result in better things for you? Imagine a world where you didn't run away from your problems or try to avoid conflict at all costs. The don't quit mantra is about embracing change and using your substantial potential to overcome any and all of the challenges that are placed in your path.

In this scripture, I've found great solace—it speaks of the things that can be achieved if you put your faith in God and use your many talents that were specially chosen for you. Failure is a manmade concept that has no real meaning for people with potential. Potential, courage, and faith drive you forward until your goal is achieved.

There is no such thing as "failing" to achieve something if you try your best. There can be times when you miss the mark and need to reassess your plans—but take failure out of the equation to give yourself a break. Quitting is the only real failure in this world. Until you quit, you have every chance of succeeding.

Leading a "Don't Quit" Lifestyle

Living a "don't quit" lifestyle is one of the most important changes you can make in your life. When I host seminars, I speak at length about switching from a passive attitude to an active attitude. Take charge of the way that you perceive yourself and your life.

To lead a "don't quit" lifestyle, you need to need to understand some basic truths about life that perhaps have eluded you until now:

> ➤ Without action there can be no motivation—without motivation there can be no action. Think of motivation as a rolling stone, gaining momentum every time you push on it. If you don't act, the stone will eventually stop. Becoming a doer is just like that. You have to be

motivated, and continue the motivation by pushing that stone as hard as you can, whenever you can. Don't quit!

- The perfect time for change doesn't exist. It's always amazed me how people can wait for things to happen in their lives. They wait for the perfect time to get married, or have kids, or to start a new job. Wake up! There is no such thing as the perfect time! Your "don't quit" lifestyle begins now. There is no need to wait for that non-existent perfect time.
- I'm not going to quit, and these excuses are just excuses. People love to excuse away their behavior or attitudes. There's a good REASON why I haven't been able to be successful. These reasons are no more than mental constructs—a way to excuse how you gave up on your goals before you made them a reality. In my "don't quit" lifestyle, there are no good excuses.
- Time takes time. Success, happiness, and all of those good, desirable concepts are what you want in your life. But they take time. Imagine a house being built over a period of six months. It begins with the foundation, then brick, then plaster. Months go by and eventually—with the fixtures and paint in place—you have something that resembles a home. It took time, just like your eventual success will take time, to go through the building phases.
- Risks are a deterrent when you're trying to live a "don't quit" lifestyle. But there is nothing in the world that you can't handle and overcome. We were made to meet challenges head on and win. One defining characteristic of the human spirit is our inability to ignore risks. We are courageous, strong, and daring—

it's why we have evolved so quickly. In you is the ability to take on any obstacles and destroy them.
- ➤ Finally, leading the "don't quit" lifestyle is about closing off those escape routes we all like to give ourselves. "I'm going to try and lose weight" is not the same as "I'll lose ten pounds." The first leaves room for escape. If you're going to do something, set that goal and then do it. It's that simple. There's no escape; there is no failure. You'll just keep working at it until it's a success.

Five Ways to Overcome Anything

You have the power to overcome anything the world throws at you. Yes, you do! 1 Corinthians 10:13 says, *"No temptation has overtaken you that is not common to man. God is faithful, and he will not let you be tempted beyond your ability, but with the temptation he will also provide the way of escape, that you may be able to endure it."*

There is always a way to get around or destroy the obstacle in your path. Of course, this is chalked up to what you are willing to do to succeed. Here's how to overcome anything in life.

#1: Turn what disempowers you into what empowers you.

Use the FAT formula to transform obstacles into achievable goals.

- ➤ F stands for feeling – Know what you are feeling, and acknowledge it.

- ▶ A stands for acceptance – Accept your feelings, and let go of any shame or fear about them.
- ▶ Finally, T stands for transcend – Make the decision to turn this problem into a solution and to see it as an opportunity.

#2: Focus on positive thinking not negative thinking!

There is great power in positive thinking, and you'll be surprised how much easier things get when you're not battling yourself and your thoughts. Kick the negative self-talk to the curb and concentrate on the positives. Even if there is only a glimmer of hope, that's all you need.

#3: Don't be afraid to make mistakes.

Life doesn't come with a field guide, and no matter how hard you try—eventually you're going to make some mistakes. Who cares? Mistakes are learning opportunities. People that make tons of mistakes are usually the best at what they do, because they know what NOT to do. Don't ever be afraid to try new things, break the rules and make mistakes.

#4: Think about your obstacle's conditions.

Every obstacle comes with a set of conditions that can be changed. Solutions nearly always lie in these changes if we're only prepared to look for them. Because you are involved, you have the power to change environmental conditions that surround the problem in order to come up with a favorable solution.

#5: Become a total time-lord.

When you learn to master the art of time management, any obstacle can become nothing more than a blip on the radar. Set yourself time limits, goals, and more—push yourself to find solutions to the problem and set yourself a time limit to do it in. Not only is this motivating, but it often leads to better results.

These five tips will help you overcome whatever obstacles crop up in your life. But they are only tips—for them to work, you have to make them work. That means dedication, iron will, and of course, using the "don't quit" lifestyle to succeed.

Poetry and Emotion

In my years of struggle and finding out who I was—and what I wanted to do with my life—a very close friend of mine gave me a little card to keep in my wallet, and on that card was a poem called "Don't Quit"—its words still resonate with me today.

When things go wrong, as they sometimes will
When the road you're trudging seems all uphill
When the funds are low and the debts are high
And you want to smile, but you have to sigh
   When care is pressing you down a bit
   Rest, if you must, but don't you quit.

Life is queer with its twists and turns
As every one of us sometimes learns
And many a failure turns about

When he might have won had he stuck it out;
Don't give up though the pace seems slow—
You may succeed with another blow.

Often the goal is nearer than
It seems to a faint and faltering man
Often the struggler has given up
When he might have captured the victor's cup
And he learned too late when the night slipped down
How close he was to the golden crown.

Success is failure turned inside out—
The silver tint of the clouds of doubt
And you never can tell how close you are
It may be near when it seems so far
So stick to the fight when you're hardest hit—
It's when things seem worst that you must not quit.

Sometimes our emotions can get the better of us, and that's when quitting becomes such a big possibility. Being emotionally drained after facing an obstacle—or even almost facing one—can ruin your chances of succeeding. When this happens, I like to turn my eyes upwards and trust in God's strength when mine fails.

Throughout my life there have been moments of trial when I was pushed to the limit with no way out. Of course, God always helped me out of those situations no matter how dire they were at the time. As the poem says, life has many twists and turns, but you can never be sure how close you are to success until you're really pushing for it.

There's a real lesson there for passive minded people. To lead a "don't quit" lifestyle you must embrace your emotions and weaknesses and understand that they are an important part of the process. They should never derail you or distract you from your goal however. Change your mindset first, and you have every chance of breaking through those emotional barriers that keep you from success.

Your Dreams and Quitting

You'll see all sorts of advice out there in the world about following your dreams or being careful when you make decisions that involve your dreams. I believe that everyone is born with a dream in their hearts. For me, it was always about people—since I could remember, I was always fascinated with people and how they lived.

I knew from a young age that I would be a leader, helping as many people as I could. Some people aren't so lucky. They have many dreams, or their dream becomes impossible because of something physical that is out of their control. I really believe that God intends for us all to follow our dreams.

That's why He takes us down different paths in this life and equips us with certain abilities to help us along the way. Of course, so many people are too busy surviving to notice that they aren't living. The only happiness and fulfillment you're going to get on this earth is if you're living life to the max—the way God intended you to.

The first step is admitting to yourself that you have a dream. Think of yours right now. It will be that thing that you think about often and dream about—but never thought was possible. The reason you have this dream in your heart is because it is possible! You are a powerful person and can make unimaginable things happen in your life.

The death of dreams comes when people quit too early. "I tried to open a business, but it failed." You have to ask yourself—why did it fail? Did you access every available resource to keep it going and to make it successful? The sad answer is that few people truly try their best. If they do—and things still fail—it can be devastating to experience.

Instead, we as people choose to bow out while there is still some dignity left. It's NOT the right thing to do. That's running away from your dreams instead of hanging onto them for dear life. Solutions will always present themselves if you have access to all of your potential. The only way to do this is by practicing the art of "never quitting."

When you don't quit, you're literally forced to explore the deepest recesses of your potential. When it's just you up against a large obstacle, that's when we find out who we really are. Don't run away; don't quit. Face that obstacle head on, learn from the experience—and become a master at success.

The only thing that separates you from very successful people is that the successful people never once entertained the idea of quitting. It's really as simple as that—they kept going until one day the hard work and struggle paid off.

Fulfillment through Perseverance

The first time I discovered that perseverance led to fulfillment was during a class project. I had been working on this display for science class, but it turned out terribly, and I wasn't happy with it at all. I redid the display five or six times before I was happy with the end result.

The next day I took my project to class, and it was a huge success. I recognized that I wouldn't have been able to experience the huge reward if I hadn't persevered with the mechanics of the project; a small lesson, but one I didn't soon forget.

In my time as a life coach, I've found that perseverance is one of the top traits a person can hope to have. It's not something you're born with—it's something you learn. Unfortunately, many people don't learn this lesson early on in life, and instead, they learn to defend their emotions by never really trying hard at anything.

You'll find that the people who are most persistent in this world are also the most successful. People that don't try, procrastinate, and never take risks—never experience the rewards that come from living a "don't quit" lifestyle. You will find fulfillment in perseverance. I know because I've helped many clients get there over the years.

Who knew that trying hard would be such a blessing? It's the one thing that is missing in so many of our lives. If you want to be a doer and someone who never quits on success, happiness, and fulfillment—then you need to learn perseverance now.

Bad things will happen. People will pass away. Businesses fail. Dreams seem a thousand miles away. But as long as you have a voracious spirit, you're always moving closer to your dreams and your goals. Inch by inch, you'll get closer until you succeed. It's inevitable when you never stop trying—and people forget that.

If you've found your life hollow and lacking recently, perhaps it's because you have all this pent up potential and nowhere to put it. Channel your potential into perseverance, and you'll find that nothing is impossible. You could decide to become anything, do anything—and with enough drive, will, and faith—you can make it happen.

That's not a promise; that's a fact. If you continue to push, eventually the world will open up to you in ways you could never have previously imagined. What if I told you that you could have anything and be anything you want? Some people may laugh and roll their eyes. But I've seen it happen. I've made it happen!

Never discount how important leading a "don't quit" lifestyle is to your wellbeing. Reject what life has thrust upon you, and start to seize what you want from it!

[02]

Work It to Win It

"Twenty years from now you will be more disappointed by the things that you didn't do than by the ones you did do. So throw off the bowlines. Sail away from the safe harbor. Catch the trade winds in your sails. Explore. Dream. Discover."

MARK TWAIN

Before I became a life coach, I decided to enter the corporate world, and I gained 12 years of extensive cross functional expertise in performance management, business development, corporate training, and sales consulting for several international corporations. Did it make me happy? It did at the time, but I was forced to move on.

Moving, or "acting" as I call it, is not a strong point for people who are dissatisfied with their lives. These are the kind of people that say, "I have to do X for the money," or "My dream of X will never happen." Honestly, you have to work it to win it, my friend.

Your Life Under a Microscope

What does it mean to be a "doer"? In my experience, there are two kinds of people. There are those people that want something and then take action to get it and those that think about taking action but never do it. Their negative perceptions chase them away from doing anything worthwhile.

Men and women these days are terrified of living up to their potential. What if you give it your all—and you still aren't good enough? I could never think that way. My fear was always—if I don't try my best, what regrets will I have? This is a better way to frame how you live your life.

Take a moment to put your life under a microscope. Let your mind wander. Do you live where you want to live? Are you in a happy marriage? Do you have all the money you need? Have you allowed your dreams to come true? Most people will answer no to these questions. Life is just too tough to be perfect.

We say that instead of acknowledging that none of us strive for perfection. I bet, if you did, you'd get it. Can you remember why you have landed up where you are right now? I bet it's because you settled. You needed money; you had no choice. Things never turn out as planned anyway, right? Wrong!

If things haven't turned out as planned for you, it's because you stopped taking action at some point. And like I said before, this is at the CORE of all of your problems. You have to work it to win it! If you're not working towards success, you're settling for failure.

I've spoken about the invaluable act of not quitting, but without the desire to live a pro-active life, you're never going to get there. Let go of your regret, and seize the day! They aren't unlimited!

Decision Making and Success

There is one roadblock on the path to success that many people tend to overlook. That's why I'm going to hone in on it; so that you can recognize the danger signs when they happen. In the bridge that connects desire and motivation to action—there is decision.

If you are unable to make a decision, you are unable to act. Many of my clients were absolutely lost at this stage. They simply didn't trust themselves enough to take their own lives in hand and reach for change. Change, action, and living a "don't quit" life is a big decision wrapped in many smaller decisions.

There is only one thing that affects decision-making ability, and that's attitude. Your attitude determines which way your decisions go. If you have a negative outlook on life, your decisions will ultimately be in favor of the negative, or passive, influences. You want to move away from this and use a positive attitude to affect an active decision-making process.

It takes a real leader to make strong decisions. It takes an even stronger leader to first lead themselves down the right path. I never realized how lax we all are with our lives until I started working as a life coach. We shirk our responsibility and place blame on others for how our lives turn out.

We do everything we possibly can to prevent having to make any real decisions because we don't want to be to blame for our own circumstances. The punch line is that we actually are responsible, whether we like it or not. When you have no money, no dream, and no prospects, that's your own fault—believe it!

It might not feel good to admit, but it's the first step in the recovery process. Right now you're a passive spectator in your own life. It's time to gear up and walk out onto that pitch for the first time. It's time to start playing the game. It all begins with the decision-making process.

Here's how I like to make decisions in a proactive manner:

➤ Rationalize the issue
➤ Establish boundaries
➤ Consider what the right thing to do may be
➤ Take action
➤ Acknowledge all feedback for learning purposes

This is based on Drucker's five elements of effective decision-making. Walk yourself through these steps each time, and you'll have to make a decision and take action. Without action, a decision is nothing more than an intangible wish. Don't ever forget that decisions are supposed to be the green light for action—so learn to make them often.

Success is just around the corner when you are able to make fast decisions and take action immediately. To make life work for you, you have to learn to work at improving your life. Too few people do it, and it's truly the key to success and happiness.

Working on Yourself

In your work and private life, you'll find that you excel most at the things you do often. After doing your job for a few years, the tasks seem almost effortless. This is because, when you actively work on something, you become much better at it. That's when you can reach the next level of your career or use new abilities to get a promotion.

I'm often asked why it's so important to focus on something as intangible as self-improvement. Isn't this whole personal development lark just for sales? The answer is NO! Just like it's important to become good at your job or a hobby that you love, you need to work consistently on yourself if you are going to excel at life.

James 2:14–17 says, *"What good is it, my brothers, if someone says he has faith but does not have works? Can that faith save him? If a brother or sister is poorly clothed and lacking in daily food, and one of you says to them, 'Go in peace, be warmed and filled,' without giving them the things needed for the body, what good is that? So also faith by itself, if it does not have works, is dead."*

This scripture speaks about the connection between faith and action. I believe that most of us don't develop as people because we don't believe in ourselves enough. We skip the faith part, so the action part can never be taken.

What we should be doing, of course, is embracing who we are, developing who we are, and trusting in our own God-given potential.

To live a MaxOut life, you must work on yourself. Work is the key word here. And work means that you need to push yourself mentally, emotionally, and physically to be better in every way. That's how you learn; that's how you succeed. We are all locked in by the boundaries that we create for ourselves.

If we can bash through these boundaries by determining what they are and then overcoming them, there's nothing we can't do. I remember a few years back I had a real problem with weight gain, and I knew that I was being passive about it. I also knew that if I tried hard and pushed myself, I could be fat-free in a few months.

So I made a plan to get myself there, and I stuck to it. The more weight I lost, the more motivated I became. Eventually, I reached my goal weight. There was no "end," and I didn't snap back into old eating habits. There was a sense of achievement, yes, but also an urgency to honor my hard work and maintain my body shape.

Since then I have taken time every day to exercise, eat right, and be healthy. But this never would have happened if there was an end to the "diet." Personal development never ends. You can decide to embrace it, work it, and make it work for you, but you can't do it hoping desperately that one day the work will end. It never ends.

Working on Your Career and Happiness

Is it possible to be happy in your career? A client once asked me this with real concern. Her point was that, even if you do something you enjoy, it eventually becomes work, and you stop enjoying it. I responded by saying that work that makes you happy doesn't feel like work. It feels like what you would be doing if you had a day off.

This is why so many people think of work as something hard, boring, uninteresting, or laborious. There is no joy, happiness, or fun in their work. Your career should not be like this at all! If you want to be somewhere in your career, it shouldn't be for money or power—it should be for happiness. Happiness only comes from doing what you love.

Money is the root of most problems in your average household, but having a lot of money doesn't eliminate problems either. You should never believe that having lots of money means that you'll be happy—it simply isn't true. Working on your career means discovering what you were meant to do with your life.

We spend most of our lives working, so it's important that this is something you stop to consider. It's not good enough to say, "I want more cash," or "I want a promotion in the career I'm currently in." If you do some soul searching, you might be shocked to discover that you are doing the complete opposite of what would make you happy.

I once had a client who worked with stocks as a financial advisor. She was desperately unhappy and couldn't figure out why. Eventually, we discovered that her true passion was working with animals and that she had sidelined this for the more lucrative career in finance. But because of this decision, she was never happy.

Years went by, and her job became stagnant because she hated it so much. Eventually she found the courage to quit and joined the staff of an animal shelter in her area. She took a pay cut, yes, but eventually figured out an innovative way to earn more money that was part of her passion. Today she is happier and more successful than she has ever been.

Once again I stress the idea that you need to "work" on your career happiness if you're going to win in life. Too much time is spent on jobs we hate, doing mindless, soul-destroying tasks that we don't enjoy. Yet we convince ourselves it's okay because we're doing well financially or because it's what society expects of us.

Well, hosh-posh to all that! I reject society's notions of what people should and shouldn't do! We are all different, wondrous strings in God's tapestry. He has given you the key to finding pleasure in work by equipping you with talents, passions, and dreams. It's time to stop ignoring them and embrace them instead.

Working on Your Family

Family is supposed to be the most important thing in our lives. Sharing your life with people you love is one of those great experiences we all get to have. Yet so many people neglect their family or take them for granted.

The world doesn't put so high a value on family these days. Career and money come before family, along with fame, power, and even appearance. Family has landed at the bottom of the pile. But it is family that can make us the happiest we've ever been.

All families have problems, clashes, and issues. That's what families do! But like yourself and your career, if you don't work on your family dynamic, it will sour. Not spending enough time with your kids, for example, will lead to them being alienated from you. They will grow up believing that you chose distance over the chance to be close to them.

It's never okay to take your family for granted in any form. The Bible often speaks about the importance of the family unit, and we should acknowledge this even today. If you want to experience a happy family life, you have to learn to work at it. Work on your relationship with your spouse, your kids, your in-laws, your parents, and your other family members.

Even though no emphasis is placed on the family as a form of happiness, it definitely is one. I know this because, when I was a child, I bounced from one foster home to the next. The dynamics in each family severely affected how I felt—about the world and about myself. You could say—when I was in a warm, loving family—I was happiest.

Don't forget that your family is the beginning and the end of your day. They will have a significant impact on your life and on your potential. If you're going to live a MaxOut life, then your family needs to be on board. The only way you're going to achieve this is by working on the ties that bind.

If there's a family member you don't talk to, for example, perhaps it's time to bury the hatchet. You'll be surprised how much emotional pressure can be released when you do the right thing. Forgiveness is a healing tonic to everyone in a family. Take some time to think about the things in your family that need work.

> Family member disagreements
> Time spent with family
> How you treat family
> The special things you all do together

If you can begin to work on the happiness in your home, then you'll go a long way to securing that success and fulfillment you've been lacking until now. There is no end to this work—but a good, clean start will get you far.

Working on Your Spiritual Wellbeing

So far, I've spoken about working on yourself, your career, and your family. There is just one more thing I want to mention—perhaps the most important of all. You can't be happy or fulfilled if your spiritual wellbeing is not acknowledged or nurtured.

We are all spiritual beings, and we crave fulfillment of the spirit just like we crave food when we're hungry. In this day and age, spirituality comes last in everything. Most people don't even bother working on their spiritual sides.

But inside you there is a hole, a desperation for something you can't quite put your finger on. This void is only filled when you spend time with God and replenish your spirit. How do you do this when the spirit is such an intangible thing? The Bible gives us the answer.

Galatians 5:22–23 says, *"But the fruit of the Spirit is love, joy, peace, patience, kindness, goodness, faithfulness, gentleness, self-control; against such things there is no law."*

It's our duty to feed our spirit by learning about and practicing these elements that strengthen our spirituality.

The scripture speaks about seeking love, joy, and a number of other things we forget about in our modern world. Instead, we are taught to seek money, fame, and power—and we wonder why none of us are happy! You can't be happy if you're not filling that void with good things.

That's why working on your spiritual wellbeing is crucial if you want to MaxOut your potential. Nothing is more motivating or fortifying than knowing God is with you every step of the way. How often do you work on your spirituality? What is your relationship like with God? Perhaps you could be doing more—a lot more.

Going to church, for example, feeds the spirit because you are able to share in God's love with his community and enjoy the fellowship of other ignited spirits. When you isolate yourself from other Christians, you take away an important way of replenishing and fuelling your spirituality.

Take a moment right now to think about the ways in which you could reignite your faith and work on expanding and improving your spirituality. Here are a few things I like to do when I feel like my spiritual wellbeing needs a boost:

- Read scriptures from the Bible.
- Really pray for things that matter in your life.
- If you feel pulled to serve or express the fruits of the spirit, do so.
- Volunteer or help people.
- Spend some quality time worshipping God.

There are many others ways that you can boost your spirit. These are just a few methods that I use to keep my spirit in tip-top shape. You'll be surprised how much happier you feel when you acknowledge your spiritual health.

[03]

Got Game? Know Who You Are!

"...if you don't have peace, it isn't because someone took it from you; you gave it away. You cannot always control what happens to you, but you can control what happens in you."

JOHN C. MAXWELL

There are 50-year-old people out there that still don't know who they are or what they want from life. In order to find your "true North," you have to develop a profound respect for self-discovery and the endless quest to discover who you are in this world.

When you know who you are—you got game! It's the same as managing a sports team. If the coach doesn't understand the characters, strengths, and weaknesses of the players, how is the coach ever going to optimize their gameplay? You need some time with you.

What Are Your Unique Talents?

You may be aware of some of your talents but not all of them. In fact, in my experience, people tend to cling to one talent in particular and define themselves by it. But we are all given multiple talents from God that we can use to live an incredible life.

I believe that God intended it to be this way, but he gave us all a choice. We are equipped with the right gear, but it's up to us to plot our own routes in life. If we choose to ignore our talents, then we waste them. If we don't use our talents to the best of our ability, I believe that we are not honoring the gifts that God gave us.

You need to work on finding out what your complete set of talents is. This is a lifelong pursuit. You may be surprised to find that, if you work on it, you can be an incredibly effective public speaker. You may find that, if you develop the skill, you can also be an amazing musician. The sky is the limit!

We forget that life is all about discovery and trying new things. That's why we lose so much of our hope for the future. We get stuck in ruts and feel like we are doomed to live these awful, uneventful lives forever. But it's simply not true, and it's not what was intended for us.

What are your unique talents? Take a moment to list them all, as many as you can. These talents form the basis of who you are. When you understand yourself, the route to happiness isn't far behind. You'll then be able to live a MaxOut life, where your potential is constantly challenged, and you feel fulfilled each and every day.

It begins with you acknowledging that you are incomplete. There is still so much more in your life that you have to discover. Never settle, and never be okay with what you have! There is always more to life and so much to experience.

How to Use These Talents for Success

Some people say that it's not enough to just have talent in order to be successful. In a way, they're right. But if you don't know what your talents are, you won't be in the right place, working on the right things, anyway. This nearly always ends up in failure.

God wants you to use your talents so that you can experience real joy in life. Once you've come to understand yourself and what you are capable of, you'll see just how powerful you are. Using your talents, you can make it all the way to the top of your chosen field.

Matthew 5:14–16 says *"You are the light of the world. A city set on a hill cannot be hidden. Nor do people light a lamp and put it under a basket, but on a stand, and it gives light to all in the* house. In the same way, let your light shine before others, so that they may see your good works and give glory to your Father who is in heaven."

This scripture speaks about your talent and how you should let it shine out from you like a light, illuminating your life path. Other people should be able to experience or benefit from your talent as God intended. When you use your talents well, you are giving glory to the Lord, who gave them to you.

But what about success? I've found in my multifaceted career that success tends to follow happiness and not money or power or anything else. When you are able to use your talent to do something you truly love, that's when success is drawn to you.

I would encourage you to use the talents you have as often as you can and to continue developing them so that you are able to achieve amazing things. It's when you allow yourself to reach for the top that you can really begin to live. That's what maxing out your potential is all about—pushing yourself to squeeze every last drop of success and happiness from life.

You already know that being passive and complacent doesn't work for you. Look at where you are right now. You're not satisfied with your life! And why should you be? You've been taught to ignore the most crucial parts of it.

Your success hinges on your ability to unleash your talent on this world. We are all blessed with varying degrees of talent. For some people, international fame may be what is required to be happy—for others just making their friends and family happy is enough. You need to figure out how far your talent can take you, and then sprint to the finish line.

Empowering Yourself

It's not easy to empower yourself when you've lived in a world that has taught you to devalue your abilities at every turn. Confidence is a concept we throw around a lot, but who doesn't suffer from a little bit of doubt now and then? Being an empowered person is vital to living a MaxOut life.

You will be feverishly pursuing your potential, expanding it and developing it in ways you never dreamed about—and this is going to require some sticking power. I used to live in a world of "I can't," and I had to learn to remove this phrase from my vocabulary.

There is no such thing as "I can't." Instead of saying you can't lose weight, say "I know the method for losing weight, but I struggle to stick to the eating plan." This clarifies that it's not something you can't do but a problem that needs to be solved. Obviously, in this instance, you need a better or simpler eating plan. Then perhaps you can!

Being an empowered person is all about confidence and self-belief. When you believe that you can achieve something, it's so much easier! Better yet, because you are empowered, others will believe in you as well. This will further boost your confidence and allow you to express your talent in interesting ways.

Nobody knows you better than you know yourself. If you trust yourself enough, you'll begin to truly understand what you can and can't achieve. It may scare you to discover that—if you really wanted to—you could be the best, I mean the very best, in the world. Why wouldn't you give yourself the chance to experience that?

Too often talented individuals are torn apart by self-doubt, and it's got to stop. Doubt is a dream killer and will keep you from reaching your full potential. I'm not even sure that there is such a thing as full potential—because if you work at it, your potential never stops increasing. That's why I know, if you really wanted to, you could do anything.

Empowered people rule this world because they tap into that special talent and ability that God has given them. No one that becomes really successful ever knows that their plans are going to work out. They believe in themselves and act on faith.

Steve Jobs had no idea his inventions would one day make him a billionaire. He began alone in his home, like you are now. The difference between you and Steve is that he was a naturally self-assured man. He knew of his talent, and he used it daily.

If you dedicate your life to pushing the envelope and discovering what or who you are, you'll be amazed at the result. Your talents can take you places, but you have to believe in yourself first. Empower yourself to do this!

Getting Game If You Need Some

I know who I am, even though it took me a long time to discover it. I got some serious game. What that means is that I know what I can do, where I'm headed, and how I'll deal with obstacles as they arise. I've tested my mettle, and I believe in my abilities.

How many people can say that? I mean, that really should be something we all acknowledge in primary school already. Unfortunately, instead we are told that success is about the material things that you own, the money that you have, and the stage in your corporate career that you can climb to.

Getting game is not about any of those things. How are you even supposed to make the right decisions when you don't fully understand who you are or where your talents can take you? I'm here to tell you, you've had it all wrong. Game is about happiness and fulfillment. Success is just a by-product of walking along your destined path.

I know this is true because I've done both. I tried to live a normal, mediocre life with a job at a pharmaceutical company, a family, and a decent income. I wasn't happy! It always felt wrong, like something was missing. I think I even felt guilty because I knew what I was meant to do and chose to ignore it.

The moment I quit and started working with people was the best decision of my life. As it turns out, my calling was to help other people discover their calling and inner potential. That's how I know you are meant to live a MaxOut life. You've barely brushed the surface of your potential—there's still so much life you have to live!

Getting game begins with self-examination. If I had to ask you to give me three words that describe you completely right now, would you be able to do it? Most people can't because they just don't know themselves well enough.

It would be a shame for you to become inspired by this book only to side-line what really matters. YOU are the master of your life and the Captain of your own destiny. I got game because I work on myself relentlessly, discovering new things every day. Don't you think it's time that you spent some time with yourself?

Shut out what other people want from you—your spouse, your kids, your boss, and your friends. People will always want you to be something you aren't. The real challenge in life is being yourself despite these influences. It's the one thing so many people get wrong.

So stop messing around with your life, and get game! Know who you are, and let's get down to the adventure of living your ideal life.

10 Questions to Help You Understand Yourself

I find it useful to work through a range of questions to get your mind working and moving in the right direction. Here are 10 questions that you need to answer so that you can begin the self-discovery process.

1. Look deep into your heart and consider who you are and how your talents have defined you. What are your three core talents that define you as a person?
2. Think about the hardest thing that you've ever had to do—did it expose any of your strengths, talents, or weaknesses? List them here.
3. What do other people say about your talents? Are there any traits that they comment on that you don't consider talents but actually are?
4. What are the things in this world that make you the happiest? Can you list at least ten of these things and try to find themes in what you've written down?
5. What are your beliefs, and how did you settle on them? At what point did you decide what is right and what is wrong? In other words, what is your belief system?
6. Are you happy with yourself as you are now, or do you live in a future that you aren't working towards?

7. If you could change your life in any way, how would you change it and why? Do you think it's possible for these changes to happen?
8. When you were growing up, which talents shone from you the most? Are these still your dominant talents, or do you have new talents?
9. Imagine your perfect career, with all the recognition, money, and happiness that goes with it. What has prevented you from reaching out and securing this life for yourself?
10. Do you do enough for yourself in your life, or are you too concerned with others? We all have a path to walk, and you should be walking yours.

These questions should help you understand not only who you are but how you have sabotaged your life and derailed your potential. But don't worry! It's never too late to be who you might have been—that's a fact.

It's also never too late to discover new talents. Even if you are overwhelmed with life and work, family and duties—you should find time for yourself. Your individual happiness is the most important thing in life—and while it's made up of several factors—the largest of all are potential and purpose.

Planning for Strengths and Weaknesses

We are all born with strengths and weaknesses that make us human. These keep us grounded and humble, and they allow us to grow as we overcome the impossible and triumph over fear and doubt.

Jeremiah 17:10 says, *"I the LORD search the heart and test the mind, to give every man according to his ways, according to the fruit of his deeds."* I love this scripture because I've found it to be so true over the years.

God rewards those that approach life with open arms because they are living as he intended. We were never supposed to be born, go to school, get a job, have a family, and then suddenly be successful. This is not success. Real success is all about finding out who you are and what you can achieve in this world.

And that means planning for your strengths and weaknesses. I define these two traits like this:

> *Strengths:* The traits that help you excel with your talents
> *Weaknesses:* The traits that hinder your progress with your talents

You need to watch out for these traits, and they can help you or derail you on your journey of self-discovery. If you are a singer, for example, a strength may be stage presence; a weakness—stage fright. You will have to learn to overcome the stage fright in order to be the best at what you do—singing.

This obstacle can result in two things—either you give up on your dream because the stage fright gets the better of you, or you smash through it with your outstanding stage presence and excel. It's a decision that each of us make when we come across an obstacle.

That's why you need to be able to recognize your strengths and weaknesses in relation to your talents. These are the features in your life that will either spur you on or hold you back. But identifying them is half the battle. If you know you procrastinate a lot, you can combat this by implementing more plans of action by goal setting.

Take a moment to think about who you really are. What strengths do you rely on to get by in your daily life? What weaknesses do you fall prey to? Just like talents can be developed, so can these traits. You can grow your strengths and reduce your weaknesses if you can recognize them.

Then you can use these traits to become better at your chosen talents. Remember that talent is the ability, not the action. Action is dictated by your strength or weakness in an activity. You may be a great singer, but if you never put yourself on stage, no one will ever hear you. That's why you need to be mindful of these elements.

[04]

Embrace the Transformation Process

"The power behind taking responsibility for your actions lies in putting an end to negative thought patterns. You no longer dwell on what went wrong or focus on whom you are going to blame. You don't waste time building roadblocks to your success. Instead, you are set free and can now focus on succeeding."

LORII MYERS

Chances are you're nowhere near where you'd like to be in your life. I believe that a very large reason for this is that, along the way, you became a negative self-talk master. You are your own harshest critic, and over the years, you've put a stop to your potential—because of things you've tried and failed or things that haven't worked out as planned.

Something I learned when I was very young was that you can plan the destination, but you can't plan the route you take to get there. There's no such thing as a spiritual GPS system! Newsflash! You STILL have the same amount of potential as you had when you were 19. You've just paused the transformation required to be who you want to be.

The Power of Positive Thinking

It's time for you to throw away the negative self-talk and become a master of positive thinking. It may seem easy—but it's the one thing that requires near super-human powers of dedication, even more so than a fad diet! It's time to ease up on yourself. When you change "I can't" into "I can," the world opens up for you.

Romans 12:2 says, *"Do not be conformed to this world, but be transformed by the renewal of your mind, that by testing you may discern what is the will of God, what is good and acceptable and perfect."* God never intended you to give up on yourself, yet that's what you did—that's what most people do.

We learn at a young age that to give up is easier than failing. What we aren't told is that giving up IS FAILING. If the world seems small and doors are closed to you—it's because you have sealed yourself off. You can't change the world, but you can change yourself! It all begins with positive thinking.

You've heard it before, but approaching life with a positive attitude really makes things happen for you. I've seen it over and over in my clients' lives. God gave you the talents you have, and to do right by them, you need to be a positive person. Negativity weighs heavily on the shoulders of unrealized potential. It crushes your spirit.

The good news is that positive thinking can become a habit—as infectious as negative thinking. There is real power in meeting the world head on with an eagerness to be challenged. We are put on this earth to find out who we are. This becomes impossible when you dissolve into a negative, self-hating person.

How Positive Thinking Can Transform Your Life

Positive thinking changed my life. My parents abandoned me at the age of six months, and I went into foster care. I remember asking God what bad things I had done to deserve such a difficult life.

It was only after walking my own path some years later that I realized we ALL have our challenges to face. Each one of us is put here to overcome, to seek a higher truth or purpose by trusting God and being the best version of yourself DESPITE your circumstances. It's easy to give up, to blame yourself, and to be bitter about an unrealized life.

It's not easy to stand up and say, "No more!" From today on, I will be a positive thinker! We all come to this decision at some point. That niggling feeling that something is wrong or that something went wrong with your life is there for a reason. It has! Things have gone wrong! But it's nothing a new look at positive thinking can't fix.

Remember, John 14:27 says, *"Peace I leave with you; my peace I give to you. Not as the world gives do I give to you. Let not your hearts be troubled, neither let them be afraid."* God tells us throughout the Bible that—if we only follow our destined paths and give him the glory—we will be blessed with success and fulfillment. It's a promise God made to us.

The irony is that I've seen this promise come true in all age groups. I've seen a client beat cancer with a positive attitude and trust in God. I've seen a 43-year-old woman recommit her life to maxing out her potential—and great things have happened for her. God does not make empty promises. We forget that. We forget our circumstances are our own fault.

Positive thinking can transform your life if you let it. Begin by practicing these exercises:

- Ignore the negative things people say about you. You know who you are and what you're capable of. With God's help, everything is possible.
- Don't criticize yourself anymore. Replace negative words with positive ones when you speak to your inner self. The world is harsh enough without being down on yourself.
- Smile whenever you get the opportunity; it helps you think positively.
- When you think negative thoughts, identify what they are and how they affect you. "I'm a failure," for example, puts you down and has no function in your vocabulary.
- Begin expecting the best out of situations, and good things will begin to happen. Let God's light shine from you, and bring positivity to others.

As bad as things are for you right now, they can be great again—if you allow it. Only you can fire up your transformation again. But it wants to happen! You have everything inside you that you need—except confidence, faith, and a positive outlook.

Becoming Who You Are

It's strange realizing for the first time that you've been living in a life of your own making. I thought for the longest time that I was just a product of my upbringing, the result of poor parenting and the harsh economy. But this is passing the buck in a big way. You can't blame the world for who you are.

There will always be people better off and worse off than you. Life is not about comparisons, even though we are taught in school to "keep up with the Joneses." There is something far more difficult going on—an inner battle that you can only win if you understand the rules. No one explains these rules to us, so we give up. We settle instead of succeeding.

God put us all on this magnificent earth so that we could become who we are. We're not only a collection of the experiences that we have here on earth; we're living, breathing potential that hasn't been realized yet. So few people get to realize who they really are. They don't even begin the transformation process because they don't see any value in it.

God created us in his own image—by nature we are all creators. That's why we long for more, even when we don't know what is missing. Deep down, unrealized potential is like a shard of glass in your arm. It's not going to affect you now, but as time goes by, it becomes more painful to bear. Then we develop guilt, and doors begin to slam shut.

When did you stop trying? When did you stop working on yourself? I know how easy it is to become distracted by life, bills, family, kids, work, and more work. Surviving is hard enough without having to deal with the additional burden of being a positive person. But it's a transformation step that you're going to have to take.

Until now, you have been the antagonist in your own epic story. While you think you are the victim, you've actually been the villain. Villains do everything in their power to lead heroes off the path, to make them ignore or sacrifice their destinies. You've been doing this to yourself. It's what has held you back all these long years.

But enough of that! It's time to embrace transformation and to become the hero in your story. Begin by ridding yourself of that villain/victim mindset—it does nothing but bring you down. When it's you against the world, you'll succeed! But you have NO chance of succeeding if it's you against yourself.

Becoming who you are is a process. Yes, you've wasted time. Yes, you aren't perfect. Luckily, there is no age limit on when your potential ends. As long as you choose to change, you can do it. Stop hiding away, and let's MaxOut your potential!

10 Positive Thinking Mantras

One technique that I like to use to kick-start the positive thinking process is to get my clients to recite positive mantras or affirmations every day. Giving yourself some positive reenforcement every day is just what you need to begin seeing the world in a different light.

1. When I believe in myself, other people believe in me as well.
2. Today I'm going to open my heart and allow wonderful things to happen in my life.
3. I will find the positive viewpoint in everything I do, see, or speak about.
4. Today I will choose to have positive thoughts over negative ones.
5. No one controls what or how I think but me, and I choose to think positively.
6. I am a calm, confident, self-assured person eager to live my life.
7. I will only think about things that create balance and harmony and that motivate me to be better.
8. Everyday my thoughts become more and more positive, which will help me get to where I need to be.
9. My optimism improves my life, while negativity makes it harder.
10. I'm living this life to MaxOut my potential, not hide from it.

Affirmations are often misused, or they feel silly when you're doing them. That's because people misunderstand the reason for using mantras like these. An affirmation is not meant to be used to improve your moods. It's supposed to be a way to slowly, gradually change the way that you think by inviting the conscious mind to store these positive statements in the subconscious.

If you say something enough times, you begin to believe it—that's human nature. Don't believe me? Think about something you're terrible at. Why are you really terrible at it? I bet it's not because you spent years trying to be the best at it! It's because you had an experience and began to tell yourself you were awful at it. So, you became awful.

This is what happens with most things in our lives. We choose what we like and what we don't like, what we'll be good at (because it comes easily) and what we're terrible at (because it's hard). I'm still a firm believer in the idea that anyone can be brilliant at anything if they do it often enough. And that's what positive affirmations are for.

Saying positive things will result in positive thought processes and, eventually, positive actions. That's just how things work. So, if you feel silly saying these affirmations, remember—this is a proven psychiatric technique.

Stick with it, and it will work for you. One day you'll wake up and FEEL the way you've always wanted to. It will be because you stuck with the affirmations, and they seeped into your subconscious mind.

Mistakes Are Learning Opportunities

We all make mistakes; after all, we're only human. Or perhaps there's another way to think about mistakes. How about, "We all make mistakes because we're human." Even though we aren't taught to believe it, mistakes are one of the truly magical things about this life. Every time we make a mistake, we grow as people.

Until now, mistakes have been lethal to your destiny. They have disturbed you so much, and hit you so hard, that you've forgotten what their purpose is. Mistakes don't exist to make you feel small, incompetent, or worthless. They exist to help you build the skills you need to overcome your next big obstacle.

Life is a series of these obstacles stacked together—one after the other standing in your way. The mistakes that you've made have ruined your self-esteem and stalled your personal growth. The most successful people in the world have also made the most mistakes—did you know that? The only difference is they learned from their mistakes.

Learning from a mistake doesn't mean avoiding the consequences of making another mistake. We must all make mistakes! I make several every day. A wise businessman once told me, "You can't know what to do until you know what not to do." Life is a sequence of finding out what not to do. But we get scared and feel exposed. Then we hide.

Isaiah 41:10 says, *"Fear not, for I am with you; be not dismayed, for I am your God; I will strengthen you, I will help you, I will uphold you with my righteous right hand."* There are passages like this all throughout the Bible, and it's because God knows how difficult life can be. In times of doubt and despair, we're supposed to rely on Him, not ourselves.

Of course, if we look at ourselves, we'll lose hope. Who are we to expect great things? How would we ever make them happen? Alone, it's impossible. Luckily, we're not alone. From the moment we are born, God is there, ready to help us along our destined paths. We just forget to ask him for help.

Mistakes are learning opportunities, and if you're not learning, then you're not transforming. That's why you feel so stagnant in your life right now. We were never meant to settle for things that we don't want! You have God, the creator of all things, on your side—and you've chosen to sit out of the game! People wonder why they're unhappy.

I mention mistakes because this is where most negative self-talk happens. But it doesn't have to be this way! Consider the life-long implications of making mistakes, and you'll be on the right path. No more, "I'm a failure." Instead say, "This mistake taught me not to X. I am one step closer to success."

Transform and MaxOut!

The word "transform" literally means to make a marked change. I can't stress enough how important positive thinking is for your future transformation. You have to change the negativity inside so that you can affect positivity on the outside. Maxing out your potential will consist of a series of mistakes that will never end. Embrace it!

Life is about learning, breaking through boundaries, and discovering the person inside yourself that is so unique and special that God brought you into this world. You've forgotten how incredible life can be because you've allowed yourself to get caught up in the insignificant details, the fear, and the disappointment.

That's why I've taken the time to write this book. People walk around in misery, not understanding where it all went wrong for them in their lives. I can tell you! The moment you gave up on transformation and maxing out your potential was the moment you gave in. From there, negativity dug you a deep, dark hole that you've been living in ever since.

The good news is that this hole can be filled. This void in your life that has made you so unhappy and so unsatisfied can be transformed. You've forgotten what a powerful person you can be. But it's not too late! This is just the beginning for you. No matter how old you are, it's never too late to be your ideal self.

So what do you say we get moving on your transformation! You've done the worst thing already that you can do in life—forget about your God-given purpose. That's one mistake that you can really learn from. Now, it's time to try it the other way. When you're maxing out your potential and living each day as the person God made you, your life will change.

Abundance, success, and happiness come when you are being true to yourself and honoring God by using the gifts he gave you. We can't all be missionaries, prophets, and pastors. But we can serve God by enriching the world with who we are. This is the transformation story that you want.

The MaxOut program is going to push you and ask you to take a really hard look at your life. There will be moments where you feel sad, happy, or inspired. Take a moment to mark the time when you decided to step back onto the path that God laid out for you. Then realize that the power to achieve these dreams has always been inside you.

Life is hard, but it was never meant to be miserable. An army that continually retreats from the battlefield will always lose confidence in their fighting ability. The key here is to ready your charge. Life is a battlefield, and it's time that you fought back for your own sake.

[05]

Courage in Your Career

"We gain strength, and courage, and confidence by each experience in which we really stop to look fear in the face...we must do that which we think we cannot."

ELEANOR ROOSEVELT

No one dreams of becoming an industrial operations manager for a textile company when they're a child. Yet the world is brimming with jobs that we've never even heard about. Every now and then I'll meet someone, hear about their work, and think, "How can you possibly be happy doing that?" The truth is that work isn't about happiness; it's about money.

We've all made that compromise—you reach an age when you realize that money is everything, and then you fall into a career or job that gets you the most you can. That's not what God intended. You are supposed to take pleasure, satisfaction, or joy in your work—and that only comes if you're passionate about your career.

Where Your Career Is Right Now

You have a career, and whether you've been working in this career for one year or ten, at some point you decided that this was the way you were going to earn money. I can't believe how much job dissatisfaction there is in the world. People become severely depressed because they are forced to work in positions they hate because they have debt.

Worst of all, I've heard some horror stories about the people my clients have worked with, all in the name of earning money. We pigeon ourselves into corners because we become convinced that "this" is as good as it's going to get. The news says jobs are scarce. People are losing their homes and belongings. You're lucky to have a job!

It's amazing the excuses that we make for ourselves. What we don't consider is who we are and how that changes things. Because you're you—and you're great at what you love—the job market doesn't matter; you'll always be able to find a job. But you don't because the risk is too much, and you just don't believe in yourself like you should.

Are you even in a career that you enjoy? Most people can't agree to that. They know roughly what they love to do, but they can't figure out a way to make money from it. So, they become drones in a workforce, slaving away at jobs they hate for money they never get to enjoy. If you aren't careful, the working world will chew you up and spit you out.

Even if you do enjoy parts of your job, I bet you're not as far as you'd like to be in the organization. It's because you actively hold yourself back. Is this what you want for your career? Do you really want to work day in and day out for nothing but money? At the end—when you retire—you'll look back and regret the time you wasted.

Where Your Heart Lies

Now ask yourself this incredibly difficult question. Where does your heart lie? What is it that you think about because it's fun and you enjoy it? What do you do purely because you love doing it? Perhaps this is your calling and not the career you're currently maintaining. Every day you work in a job you don't enjoy is a day you can never get back.

Most of my clients have one response when I ask them why they choose to stay in jobs that they hate. It boils down to fear. You can't allow yourself to be afraid of things that haven't happened yet. You're afraid of losing your house, not paying the rent, and not paying your accounts, your car, your phone, and your food bills.

There are SO many debts that you simply can't ignore. Would it be right to say that you work every single day for next to nothing? Most of your money is going to debts and bills. What little you have left is usually spent impressively quickly. You get no satisfaction from your work or from the money it provides.

Your plan of working for money is not working out. And this never ending fear is keeping you shackled to a career that is slowly consuming your life. We spend most of our time working while we are on this earth. To me, that means wasting one minute in a nightmarish job is not an option. Life is not about compromising who you are for money. That's what you've been doing!

Psalm 27:1 says, *"The LORD is my light and my salvation; whom shall I fear? The LORD is the strength of my life; of whom shall I be afraid?" I feel like anything is possible, as long as God is on your side—which is always! We forget that God tells us not to fear and that he will look after us.*

That means not being afraid that, if you leave your career, you'll end up broke. It means having the faith required to free yourself from the mental bonds of career slavery! Money is all over the place, and you know what? You make more of it when you're doing something you love. That's a well-known fact.

Yet people continue to live in fear, going to their horrible jobs and hating their lives because they have no faith in themselves or in the promises God has made them. You can be and do anything. The only thing stopping you is a lack of courage.

Like it or not, happiness comes at a cost—and that cost is the ability to be courageous about the decisions that you make. Choose happiness over money. Put your faith back in God, and stop living in perpetual fear!

The Courage to Work to Win

I read somewhere once that courage is not the absence of fear but the ability to overcome it. And while we think of courageous people as superheroes, we forget that courage begins and ends in the mind. The quality of your mind or spirit determines how courageous you are. It's no wonder you've been stuck in a job you don't enjoy!

When you settle, it erodes your strength of mind and passionate spirit. Because of the decision you made to place money above your own happiness, you took something from yourself and have felt the loss ever since. The moment you conceded, you gave up on your potential. Now you need to find the courage to use it again.

I like to think of courage as something you can learn. It's about taking those uncomfortable risks and believing beyond all hope that you will make it work. Having faith in yourself and in the gifts that God has given you is your greatest source of courage.

Matthew 7:7 says, *"Keep on asking, and you will receive what you ask for. Keep on seeking, and you will find. Keep on knocking, and the door will be opened to you."* In this scripture, we're taught a very important lesson in perseverance. No one starts out being what they want to be—it takes long years, trials, failures, and successes to get where you want to be.

It's not enough to find the career that will reignite your passion for life. You need to be the best that you can be in this career. It's only when you play to win that you win. You need to have the courage it's going to take to do that. Success is hard earned. No one's going to pat you on the back for it. It's something you have to do for yourself.

When you finally find the courage to work to win—that's when lives change. For me, it wasn't only about being a life coach and public speaker. It was about being the absolute best version of a life coach and public speaker that I could be. And it took work! It still takes work! But I have the courage to work for what I want in this brief life.

I've spoken with CEOs that earned six digit salaries and were miserable. One of my clients spoke at length about this emptiness inside that they can't get rid of. I told her about courage and what God wants for each of us—to live that MaxOut life. She confided in me that she only ever wanted to be a ski instructor. It was her passion.

A few years on and my client now owns a Christian ski lodge up North. She retired from her corporate position at the age of 42 and now works as a ski instructor. It was a very long, hard battle to learn the ins-and-outs of running a lodge, but she's never been happier. And it's because she finally placed her own happiness first.

Taking Leaps of Faith

What is it like to take a leap of faith? Well, it's scary. Most people don't trust themselves enough to become someone who is willing to act on faith. Instead, they make excuses and fold themselves in fear until the very idea of taking that leap is impossible to them. Imagine if I could guarantee your success if you took that leap!

I'm sure a lot more people would be willing to leap if they had some guarantees. And that's essentially the difference between people that live with courage and those that live in fear. With a fearful mindset, you expect the worst to happen.

Your endeavor will fail; you'll lose all of your money, your home, your car, and your lifestyle.

People with a courageous mindset don't think this way. They expect the best to happen—and MORE—they work relentlessly until they make it happen. This is because they understand that success is a process and that you can only fail if you give up. To them, a leap of faith is nothing more than a promise they make to themselves— not to fail.

And for me, that's as good as a guarantee. It's no wonder people with positive mindsets tend to do better in business. They are willing to take more calculated risks, and they aren't blinded by unimportant things. Money is not their primary concern. It's just something that happens when they are doing what they love to do.

Taking leaps of faith requires you to be fearless—to trust in yourself and in God—and to believe with all of your might that you will make it work. It's funny how we aren't prepared to leave our comfort zones, yet these zones are never that comfortable. In fact, they are often quite terrible and shouldn't be called comfort zones at all.

To take a leap of faith is to be courageous. To take many is to MaxOut your potential. You want to be the person who is able to take sweeping leaps of faith in the name of your happiness, your path, and your journey in life. Right now, you're not that person. You're the person who does the same thing every day, wishing your life would change.

You spend most of your time working in a job you really don't enjoy because you "have" to. You've lost faith in yourself, and it shows. No one should have to live an unfulfilled life. You are worth more than that. Decide that this will be your first big leap of faith. You're going to read this book and take its lessons to heart. Then you're going to practice these lessons.

It's going to take a lot of courage to eventually leave your old career behind. But this is something you must do. If you don't, your life will continue as it is now. And this is perhaps the biggest tragedy of all—to see change, refuse it once again, and continue living in fear of the life you have chosen.

Faith for Motivation and Success

Faith is a powerful force; one that guides and blossoms the more you practice it. In my struggle for success, I learned one unquestioning truth. Without a never ending supply of motivation, success will always be out of your reach. Motivation is perhaps one of the most difficult traits to hold onto after you've taken a leap of faith.

You could say that faith drives motivation and that motivation tests your faith. Traits like desire, ambition, dedication—these are nothing without motivation. You can want something badly, and have all the tools you need to make it happen, but if you aren't motivated to work hard so that you can change your dream into reality, it won't work.

This brings us to another conundrum. How do you stay motivated when there is no guarantee of success? Easy—you put your trust and faith in God. It begins with faith in your own ability and almost always ends with a boost from the Lord. I could never have achieved the things in my life without believing that God intends for me to be successful.

Even though faith is invisible, it's an essential ingredient in your success. It opens doorways for you that allow sudden and unexpected successes to take root in your life. When you finally start to trust in yourself, your confidence will grow. Then when you have those doubting moments, you can give them to God.

2 Corinthians 5:6–7 says, *"So we are always of good courage. We know that while we are at home in the body we are away from the Lord, for we walk by faith, not by sight." It's important to always walk by faith and not by the things that we are told to want in this world. Money has been guiding you up to this point, and not very successfully.*

Instead, find the courage inside yourself to be a person of faith. This faith will motivate you to success like nothing you've ever experienced. That defining moment when you truly believe that you can make something big happen in your life is all you need to keep you going. All at once you've discovered the secret to success—your own self-belief.

Work on your faith, and draw inspiration and motivation from it. You'll need this boost if you are to continue on a different path that leads towards your happiness and fulfillment. I'm sure inside you right now there is a dream that you've had forever; the way you wish your life had turned out. You may not be able to change the past, but you can change yourself.

Trust in God; He believes in you. If you can take the time to understand that, you can do anything. With faith on your side—you really can move mountains.

Daring to Dream

Mark 9:23 says, *"All things are possible for those who believe."* When you dare to dream about your ideal life, it comes into sharp focus. Dreaming has always given us the ability to make intangible things real. If you are able to dream about your ideal life, then you have something worth working towards.

This scripture refers to the importance of believing in God and in the abilities that he's given to you. There are few things as important in this world as dreaming, and it's vastly overlooked as a motivator. But that's exactly what it is. Not only has God given you the means to achieve your dreams, He's also given you the means of seeing what your future could be if you only take the time to believe in it.

Not many people dare to dream anymore, as so few dreams ever really come true. This, however, is the dreamers fault. The most innovative people on earth are all dreamers. But after they dream, they take action! By charting dozens of smaller ways to get there, a route is eventually planned for the dreamer to take.

Equipped with faith, motivation, and hard work, this person slowly makes their dreams a reality. They never stop; they never falter. It comes from a deep understanding that dreams only come true if you want them badly enough. You can't control things like timeframe, obstacles, money, or power—but you can control faith.

I promise you this—if you never stop working towards your dreams, one day you'll wake up inside one. Whether it's starting your own company, making things, or being the best PR person a corporate company has ever seen—each of us has our own dream to fulfill. I don't believe for one moment that they're random.

Inside every one of us, there is one lingering dream that defines who we are. It may seem impossible and downright silly—but it's there for a reason. God promises us that if we can overcome all obstacles and maintain our faith, success is always the outcome. I truly believe that, having tested the theory many times for myself.

It's time to inhale faith and exhale fear. Fear prevents you from dreaming and holds you back. Faith urges you onward, even when you have the most difficult path ahead of you. Dare to dream, now and forever. It's what makes us creators in this world. It's what allows us to be happy, simply by closing our eyes.

To MaxOut your potential in your dream career, you'll need a lot of faith, motivation, and self-belief. Never let go of who you are trying to be. You were born with the potential to make it happen if you use every ounce of your God-given talent.

06

Getting Held Back and Breaking Forward

"If you are facing a new challenge or being asked to do something that you have never done before don't be afraid to step out. You have more capability than you think you do but you will never see it unless you place a demand on yourself for more."

JOYCE MEYER

How well do you really know yourself? For example, do you realize how you're going to react when a problem arises? Life is made up of a system of obstacles that test you in every way. Whether these obstacles materialize at work, at home, in your relationship or marriage, or with your friends—they always lead to one thing: being held back.

Every goal worth setting always comes with a long list of obstacles that you have to overcome. Life, in fact, never stops throwing them your way. Sure, you can choose to ignore them and move on, or you can meet them head on and destroy them! If you want to break away from the pack, you'll need to learn to face these challenges head on.

The Obstacles in Life

Obstacles in life are what make life worth living, and here's why. Without obstacles, there can be no sense of achievement or accomplishment. If everything was simply handed to us, we wouldn't appreciate it at all. Life's little obstacles teach us important lessons about ourselves. When you avoid them, you avoid learning something new about who you are.

I wouldn't say that life is one big test because you can choose to not participate in the game—but it's certainly an area of trials for people that want to lead less ordinary lives. I think you're one of those people. When you MaxOut your potential, you'll be trying so many new things that problems are bound to crop up and attempt to hold you back.

First of all, you need to recognize why things get worse at the worst possible time. I played Division I basketball in college at the University of South Carolina. I loved basketball, and I even dreamed of going pro one day. As team captain, I was fiercely dedicated and focused on winning our games.

In my third year, everything went wrong that could possibly go wrong for one of our most important games of the year. My shooting guard hurt her ankle in practice, so I was down one player. Then three of my other players caught a bug that was going around two days before the match.

At the same time, I was having problems getting the evening off for the game at my part-time job. So, I faced three obstacles: injury, illness, and the possibility of losing my job. That game was going to make or break our season, and I wanted to win—bad. I solved all three issues, and we went on to win the game.

Drained of Your Potential

How did I win that game, you ask? I thought outside the box. I got my injured shooting guard to fill in for me at the café; I loaded the rest of my team up with health supplements and medication—and I replaced my shooting guard with a promising player who was previously playing at reserve small forward.

The lesson here? Instead of caving into the massive debacle that was happening to me, I made a plan. I fought through the problems and won the game anyway. Obstacles have a nasty way of draining every last scrap of your potential. When there is a never ending list of problems, you become fatigued, and it's only too easy to give up.

I could have given up. I could have cancelled the game or postponed it. I could have made the wrong decisions and ended up not playing with my team. But I wouldn't allow the obstacles to get in my way. I had my eyes on the prize, and I wasn't about to let life get the better of my potential.

Ephesians 3:20 says, *"Now all glory to God, who is able, through his mighty power at work within us, to accomplish infinitely more than we might ask or think."* I love this scripture because it reminds me that my potential comes from God and that he has always had a plan for me. Just like he has a plan for you!

God works through us to touch other people, you know. Because my friend worked for the first time at my job, she discovered her love for cooking and is now a fulltime chef. There was a little bump in the road, and it became an opportunity instead of a problem. I see all obstacles as opportunities.

Right now, you're probably used to life getting the better of you. Obstacles rise and ruin your day, or they take pieces of your self-confidence that you'll struggle to get back. The good thing is that no one can take your God-given potential. Obstacles can, however, erode the faith that keeps you going when you're trying to MaxOut your life.

It's the reason why, when problems happen, you groan and sulk. You don't see them as opportunities; you see them as inconveniences. Just another way life is screwing you over, right? Wrong! Have you ever wondered why things get harder the older you get? It's not because more obstacles fall into your lap; it's because you have a lower tolerance for dealing with these obstacles.

Life fatigues you and takes away your will to fight for success. If you're not careful, it will crush your spirit completely. You can't let the obstacles you face dictate who you are. Instead, reclaim your right to fight against life's little problems, and win! Find out who you are by getting the better of your problems.

Identifying What Empowers and Drains You

In my opinion, there are two types of energy in this world—energy that empowers you and energy that drains you. Energy is attached to everything—people, places, actions, even time periods. During my years as a life coach I've realized that different people are empowered by different things. The same goes for being drained.

It's important to be able to identify what empowers you and what drains you so that you can use this to your advantage. For me, I'm always thinking the most enthusiastically when I'm on the courts in my backyard, shooting a few hoops. Sport energizes and empowers me, especially when I play competitively.

When you feel empowered, you have the courage to be who you want to be—and that's no small thing. This is why it's crucial that you find a range of activities that empower you in your life. Think of a few now. Can you write them down?

They can be anything from cooking, sculpting, writing, reading the Bible, cleaning your home, blogging, helping people, and improving your skills to reading, working on something specific, inspiring others, and taking power naps. Whatever empowers you and makes you feel like you can take on the world, that's what you need to be doing more of.

We don't make enough time in our lives for ourselves. There's too much work, relationship stuff, and family. Balancing life with self-improvement can be hard. Learning what can quickly and easily pick you up when you're feeling down will give you a huge advantage. You'll be able to MaxOut your potential non-stop!

There are always two sides to any coin. Just like there are things in life that empower you, there are things that can make you feel drained, small, and unmotivated. You need to be able to identify these things so that you can remove them from your life. Certain types of people, especially, can have a draining effect.

Repetitive tasks, or being completely out of your comfort zone, also have a way of draining your energy. If you're not actively thinking, learning, or enjoying yourself, then what you're doing could be draining. Get too drained and suddenly you won't have the energy to keep up with your daily motivations. Empower yourself daily so that this doesn't happen.

If you can inspire yourself every day to be better, to work harder, and to try new things, there's no telling how far you'll be able to go in life. Avoid filling your life with things that aren't important so that you don't become drained. I always found conflict, doing things that have no real purpose, and uncooperative people always drain me the most.

Breaking Free of Your Bonds

Now that you can identify the good and bad in your life, isn't it time to separate the two? It's amazing how much we take on that distracts us from leading normal, healthy lives. I used to work sixteen hour days, cook, clean, and look after the kids every day. I was constantly burnt out, but I pushed on.

But there were many unnecessary bonds that I was imposing on myself. I made it hard to break free and pursue more important things—like happiness. Once I had realized how many obstacles I put in my own way, I de-cluttered my life. I stopped cleaning and hired a nice cleaning lady to do it for me.

My husband began cooking half the meals every week. Twice a week I took my kids to the neighbor's house, where they played for a few hours, giving me some time off. And I began to be very selective about the work I'd take on. If I could delegate it, I did. If I could refuse it, I did. I went from working sixteen-hour days to working from 8 a.m. to 6 p.m.

1 Corinthians 10:13 says, *"No temptation has seized you except what is common to man. And God is faithful; he will not let you be tempted beyond what you can bear. But when you are tempted, he will also provide a way out so that you can stand up under it."* This scripture speaks about the many bonds that form in our lives.

God promises us that there are always ways to simplify things for ourselves. Sometimes we put a lot of pressure on ourselves to do things we just don't have to do. We enslave ourselves! I know I did with my insane work and home life. You really have to take a moment to peer suspiciously at your own life.

Are there things that you can stop doing to free up some time? After all, maxing out your potential and finding happiness is the ultimate life goal. You just can't put other, pointless things ahead of it. I bet right now you're thinking, "But I need to do X!" Do you really? Or is it an obstacle that is sneakily holding you back by hogging all of your time?

It's time to break free of those obstacles that you don't even perceive as obstacles! I understand better than most just how busy a life can get. There is barely even any time to keep a marriage together—I know! But don't let the MaxOut your potential program fall away because of excuses like "I have to clean."

Sometimes the most sinister obstacles are the ones we miss. Take some time—right now—and consider the things in your life that create stumbling blocks for you. Is there any way you can improve your situation?

God's Plan for You

I truly believe that we make it difficult to discover God's plan for our lives because we fill them with unnecessary things. Jeremiah 29:11 says, *"For I know the plans I have for you," declares the LORD, "plans to prosper you and not to harm you, plans to give you hope and a future."* Not only do we invite obstacles into our lives, but we ignore God's plan.

I also believe that God, in his own divine way, has let us know in which direction he wants us to travel. We either choose to go or we choose to ignore it—sometimes not even realizing that this is our destined life path. But one thing is very clear. God definitely has a plan for you. He's had a plan since before you were born.

God has told us that his plans for us do no harm and that they're in our best interest. He also tells us that his plans for us will make us happy, bringing us hope and a future—perhaps the one we've always wanted. This is why he equipped us with specific talents, skills, and strengths.

To discover what God's plan for you may be, think about your special mix of talents. Where do you thrive? Where would you be most happy? I suggest praying about it and asking God to reveal to you what he wants with your life. The answer may suddenly become as clear as day if you only ask. God answers prayers!

Next, try and do all you can with what you already have. That means developing your skills and talents, and de-cluttering your life of obstacles like we've been talking about. Be grateful for all God has given you, but realize that there is so much more if you only reach out and embrace it.

A big part of maxing out your potential involves following God's plan for your life. You'll know it when it happens because it will bring you endless joy, lots of obstacles to overcome, and a way for you to grow as a person every day. I'm still challenged when I meet new people and hear their opinions about God, their purpose, and ultimate dreams.

For me, it's comforting to know that the creator of the universe has something great in store for me and that I'm living that plan right now. It brings with it a kind of responsibility, not only to myself but to God. After all, He's the one who gave me all of these talents. I use it as a motivator to stay on the path and to keep fighting for my ideal life.

Pray about what God's plan is for your life, and don't be afraid to listen and wait for an answer. I've had clients who have waited for a few weeks before they realized what it was they should be doing.

Following Your Desired Path

I know that when you follow your desired path—and it aligns with God's plan for your life—that's when true happiness is found. After all, no one knows you better than God. He created you—from your outward appearance to the weird quirks that make you unique.

Psalms 37:4 says, *"Delight yourself in the LORD and he will give you the desires of your heart."* On my MaxOut journey of finding and fulfilling my true potential, I have drawn closer to God in many ways. I think that when you uncover a truth about yourself and place your worries and concerns in God's hands, it gives you this incredible peace that is so rare in life.

When you love what you do—and you feel like it's what you should be doing—that's when happiness becomes joy and work becomes fun. God wants each of us to experience this realization, though he leaves it up to us to find the path.

Our desired path is the path we were always meant to be on. Then life happened, and obstacles began to slowly tear your dreams apart. You stopped pushing for the life you wanted and instead settled into a life you found. This is no way to live, and it's certainly not what the Lord intended for you.

The greatest rewards come from the greatest sacrifices. To discover your path may mean you have to turn your own life inside out. You might find that you're in a loveless relationship, that you hate your job, and everything about your life seems foreign and staged. Detachment happens as a result of being so unhappy.

And as I've mentioned before, the only way to find happiness in this life is to MaxOut your potential and become who you were always meant to be. Imagine waking up excited to be alive because you are able to indulge in your passion every single day. Don't you think it's time to "uncancel" your dreams?

The final and most difficult obstacle will be determining if you will follow your desired path or not. There are many ways to pretend to follow your new path and none that result in success. The only way you're going to succeed is if you're in 100%. There is no time to waste.

If you're going to blaze your own trail and embrace your

destiny, then prepare to become someone who seizes upon challenges and defeats them on a daily basis. The moment you decide to walk on your path, the world will turn against you. Things will get harder. But if you hang in there, you can come out unscathed on the other side.

[07]

Understanding and Destroying Fear

"Expose yourself to your deepest fear; after that, fear has no power, and the fear of freedom shrinks and vanishes. You are free."

JIM MORRISON

Fear is one of the greatest obstacles that you'll face in your life. We grow up in a very fearful society, where we are taught that if you're uncomfortable with something, it's better to hide away from it than face it. But you need to understand fear in order to overcome it.

When you live your life in fear, you become someone who overlooks opportunities when they arise. Saying "no" to opportunity becomes a habit, and it's a bad one. Soon your life will feel empty because you have allowed great things to pass you by.

What Fear Does to Your Life

Fear has this uncanny way of making you avoid the things in life that could positively affect you and the people around you. This is because fear is the byproduct of other emotions, like anger, stress, pride, discouragement, and jealousy.

Joshua 1:9 says, *"This is my command—be strong and courageous! Do not be afraid or discouraged. For the Lord your God is with you wherever you go."* This scripture is an uplifting one that I like to read when I'm feeling afraid. Knowing that God walks the same path as you do is comforting, and it should give you strength.

God doesn't want us to be afraid of life, and he's very adamant about that in the Bible. Perhaps it's because there are so many things that are scary in this world. Fear is the biggest enemy because it's self-made and can stop you in your tracks.

But we don't consider the negative effects of fear very often. We believe that it's keeping us safe, when in actual fact, it's playing havoc with our lives. It's nearly impossible to live an abundant life when you are consumed by fear.

- Fear turns all answers into "I can't!"
- Fearful thoughts are designed to limit you so that you stay safe.
- Fear always comes with physical symptoms like nervousness, anxiety, and trepidation—learn to recognize these so that you can convert them into positive energy.
- Fear makes every outcome the worst possible scenario, so we start thinking the worst of every situation.
- The goal is not to rid yourself from fear but to learn to relate to fear in a different way so that you can use it to MaxOut your potential.
- When you recognize that you are afraid, you are better equipped to make conscious decisions about your life based on courage.
- Fear is meant to slow you down, but it's not meant to be used as an excuse—it has practical uses when the time is right.
- When you overcome fear, you are better able to experience beauty, love, inspiration, creativity, courage, and strength.

Fear and Potential

Fear is a potential killer. It's like a virus that infects every part of your life until there is nothing left of your dreams. It forces you to look past things that crop up in your life that may drastically change it.

It begins as a child, you know. You learn to be afraid of other people and what they think of you. You learn to do everything in your power to keep a low profile and not call attention to the fact that you're different from other people.

We go through life terrified that if we reveal what we can really do—and fail—that will make us failures.

Fear of failure is a paralyzing emotion. No one wants to feel like they're not good enough, yet this is a feeling that we come to know well by the time we are in high school. The rest of our lives are spent cautiously approaching any subject that may cause us to fail.

Fear is usually surrounded by other less pleasant feelings, like embarrassment, shame, or guilt. It's the reason why geniuses are born into the world and never do anything with their immense talent. It's the reason superstars are born, and they never step out onto the stage.

Fear can change the course of your life—just ask someone that has recently been in some form of accident or a traumatic experience. I firmly believe that everything has a balance or an opposite. You can see clearly here that fear is the opposite of finding opportunity, and it's the enemy of progress, positivity, and moving forward.

Think about what scares you the most in this world about yourself. Is it that you think you might not be good enough if you try to be who you want to be? Is it that you believe you'll fail if you ever try to go the extra mile? What is it exactly that is holding you back?

Your potential is directly related to how much fear you are able to overcome in your life. That's right! The more you free yourself from fear the greater your potential will be. This is because you'll begin to embrace all of those opportunities that you missed before.

These opportunities make it easier to learn from your mistakes and gain some great life experience. You'll grow as a person, and the world will open up to you. Don't be afraid of making mistakes—we all make them.

Don't allow fear to conquer you; it diminishes your creativity and innovative output. Only you can control how fear works within you. Use it as a motivator to break out into this world and make incredible things happen. Be afraid of going through life without ever really living it! Be afraid that you will never reach your true potential.

The Art of Overcoming Fear

Overcoming fear is an art form that you can learn any time. The best news is that the more you practice overcoming your fears the more courageous you'll become as a person. As I've mentioned before, it's better to be a courageous person than someone full of fear.

Isaiah 35:4 says, *"Say to those with fearful hearts, "Be strong, and do not fear, for your God is coming to destroy your enemies. He is coming to save you."* This is another promise from God and one of many scriptures that speaks about not being afraid.

Faith helps to diminish fear, but so do many other things:

> *Never dwell on mistakes or failures; it does nothing positive for you.* Instead, focus on the good that you got from the experience and learn from it.
> *Cut out the negative self-talk.* Don't scare yourself even more by constantly reminding yourself how scared you are or how you might fail. Only be positive about upcoming experiences.
> *To be confident, act confident.* Fear is on the inside, and one of the ways to get it out is to pretend to be confident on the outside. Your actions will help you mentally reject the fear process, and you'll begin to feel less fearful.

- *Don't be a procrastinator because procrastination promotes fear in every way.* When you're very afraid, you can't think clearly. Instead, try acting. Doing something worthwhile is a great way to overcome your fears and live with courage.
- *Most people have the same fears and desires; we're all the same.* Keep in mind that, underneath exterior fronts, most people are nice because they want to be liked. Before becoming fearful of a person, try walking a mile in their shoes.
- *Always be positive about things that are happening to you.* Even when you struggle to see the good in a situation, there will always be some good there. Look to find it, and amplify it so that you aren't afraid anymore.
- *There is no such thing as perfection, so dismiss it from your vocabulary.* If you're waiting for the perfect time, place, or person, you'll be waiting for a long, long time. Fear that acting now will ruin a perfect moment later is just holding you back.
- *Be the best version of yourself by making an effort.* Nearly anyone can improve their looks with a bit of care and the right clothing. Improve your self-confidence by looking well turned out, and you'll find you are better equipped to face fearful situations.
- *Stop comparing yourself with other people.* They honestly have nothing to do with who you are or what you can achieve. You need to compete with yourself. Outdo yourself—that's positive. Negative would be putting yourself down because you can do something as well as someone else.

The Real Meaning of MaxOut

What does it really mean to MaxOut your potential? I've been speaking about doing this throughout the book, but do you really know what it means? It means going the extra mile for yourself, not just once but every day, so that you can have a better life.

Right now we all use parts of our potential to be good in certain areas of our lives. We're great at work; we cook well; we're entertaining around people. We only use this potential when it benefits us. Yet, using this potential to its fullest is something very few people ever do. It's baffling to me how people can ignore their own talent like that.

That's why I developed the MaxOut your potential philosophy. If you're not living life to the fullest—all the time—then you're doing something wrong. We don't have an unlimited amount of time on this earth to become the best versions of ourselves.

Some people never even begin to scratch the surface of who they are. But I'll tell you this. When you do finally tap into that potential, it's life-changing. You empower yourself to find out who you are and to work on that for the rest of your life.

The real meaning of MaxOut your potential is to put fear aside and to live as if today were your last day on earth. None of us have the time to waste, yet that's all we've been doing—wasting time. It's not fair to us or to God, who created us for a higher purpose.

Your gifts are supposed to reach out and touch people, improving the world for everyone. You will only be able to make such an impact if you fully, 100%, believe in yourself and your abilities. That means removing fear from your life from now on.

As you complete this book and begin to find answers in your own life, remember this. You can't MaxOut your potential when you're afraid to put everything on the line. This isn't some lame self-improvement mantra that is going to work for a while and then stop.

It's a total revamp of your life in every way. I want you to think about the things in your life that make you afraid. Isn't it even scarier to acknowledge that, if you don't change, you'll end up wasting all of your potential on an unfulfilled, unhappy life? That's perhaps the scariest reality of them all.

If you're going to commit to this program, then you're going to need to dispel fear from your life. Don't let it get in your way. You can beat psychological fear if you realize that fear is formed through memory. Change your experience of the thing you fear, and you won't fear it anymore.

Keeping Fear at Bay

It's easy to decide now that you are going to remove fear from your life. But consider this—fear is the constant companion of progress. If things go wrong as you are trying to better yourself, fear will hit you the hardest then. You'll doubt yourself, and you'll be terrified to take another step into the unknown.

How do you keep fear at bay during these trying times?

- ▶ Face your fear, say it out loud, or write it down. Once it's out of you, you can think about it, rationalize it, and begin to reclaim the power it's taken from you.
- ▶ Use positive affirmations to dispel your fears. When you find that you are particularly afraid of something, create a good affirmation that re-enforces the positive

things you're trying to achieve.
- If perceptions are creating more fear than you can handle, change them. Think about the thing that scares you in a new way, in a positive light. Soon you'll begin to see that—in the unlikely event of this fear materializing—it won't be that bad.
- Some experts say that you should feel the fear and then do what scares you anyway. That way you let yourself know that fear doesn't control your actions—and you become stronger for it.
- Try and see the bigger picture. When you can see the overall picture—or the light at the end of the tunnel—it becomes easier to overcome your fears now. Sometimes there aren't good reasons for being afraid, but it happens anyway.
- Regrets can exacerbate fears, so it's important to try not to have too many of them. Ironically, it's usually fear that causes regret in the first place. Overcome these fears and regret less in life.
- Spending more time with God through quiet time, prayer, or at church will help you renew your faith and overcome fear. When fear becomes too much for us to handle, that's when we pass it over to the Lord.
- Stop making excuses for your fear—"I'm too tired," "It's too hard," and "I just don't have time"—these are all negative excuses. They support your fearful outlook and that mustn't be condoned.
- Keep fear at bay by practicing courage whenever the opportunity presents itself. Whether it's the courage to talk or the courage to do something you don't normally do—you'll know it when it happens.

> You are not alone. Look to your friends and family for support when you have to do things that really scare you. Public speaking for example can be terrifying. I surrounded myself with family and friends at my first public talk.

If you're going to keep fear at bay on a permanent basis, you'll quickly learn to recognize fear when it rears its ugly head. Remember, fear comes in all shapes and sizes —so don't dismiss hesitation as being natural when there are other things at work in your life.

Courage, Faith, and Strength

There are three traits I simply can't live without and three that are absolutely necessary if you want to learn how to permanently overcome fear. They are courage, faith, and strength. All three of these come from God and can be developed if you want to expand your potential.

Deuteronomy 31:6 says, *"Be strong and courageous. Do not be afraid or terrified because of them, for the LORD your God goes with you; he will never leave you nor forsake you."* Whenever I realize that fear is holding me back, I pray. I ask God to help me deal with the emotion and to not let it get the better of me.

If I'm feeling a little depleted spiritually, I'll sit down and renew my faith by reading the Bible, or I'll do another "energizing" activity that I've planned for myself. When you have more positive energy, you are more likely to overcome fear quickly.

Courage takes many forms, but to help it grow inside you, you need to recognize small opportunities in your life when practicing courage would be relevant. Going back to a shop because you've realized that they have given you the wrong change is not something everyone does.

There is that "confrontation" element that scares people away—and it's a massive hassle! But you have to be courageous and stand up for yourself, in this instance, to get the right amount of change. It means marching back into that store and saying your piece.

Faith, on the other hand, is practiced all the time, in subtle little ways. When you get on a bus without looking at where it's going—that's faith. When you commission someone to work on your landscaping while you're at work—that's faith. You need to have trust to have faith that everything will turn out as planned.

Faith is an important element in dispelling fear because it gives us hope. If we can dare to hope for a better outcome—the fear will recede. It's only when we forget to have faith that our fears grow out of control.

Finally, there is strength. I'm not talking about strength in the traditional sense but an inner strength that makes you a morally sound, upright, and ethical person. Have the strength to challenge your beliefs, to try new things, and to never allow fear to get in your way.

When you combine courage with faith and strength, you get the perfect mix for overcoming fear. If you struggle with fear—and find that you are scared of not just the big things in life but the little things as well—then you need to work on these areas.

Don't stress about it too much—God will be there, helping you along. If you can remain persistent, then you have every chance at becoming a person that never gives into fear.

[08]

Living the "I Want It All" Life

"Nothing splendid has ever been achieved except by those who dared believe that something inside of them was superior to circumstance."

BRUCE BARTON

Maxing out your potential will help you to live the "I want it all" life. From a very young age, we are taught that it's impossible to have EVERYTHING that life has to offer us. In fact, the older you become the more you are told that life isn't perfect and that you can't "have your cake and eat it too."

What this means is that we should all expect a life of compromise. But this is a negative way of thinking! When you don't expect much from life, you don't get much from it. I'm here to tell you today to renew your faith in your life. You can have it all, and all of that negative compromise stuff is just an excuse people make when they can't overcome fear.

What's Wrong with Wanting It All?

These days wanting it all means pursuing a perfect work-life balance. Why can't you express your potential to the max at work and then be a fantastic parent at home as well? There must be a way to strike the ideal balance so that no areas in your life suffer.

Yet we are told constantly that you have to sacrifice one for the other. You can either choose to have a great work life or a great home life, a good social life or a good work life. But that's all down to time management ability, isn't it?

People act like there is something wrong you with you if you aspire to "have it all" these days. I always believed that I could be an athlete, a life coach, a mom, a wife, and a really great friend—all at once. My experience in life told me that I could be.

Yet life puts fears inside your head, and you begin to think—maybe society is right, maybe I can't have it all. Then you begin to feel burnt out and exhausted, and things slow down. Suddenly you've convinced yourself that juggling a balanced life IS impossible.

But really, it's just that pesky fear that keeps holding you back. Wanting it all is a deeply personal decision, and you should not be put off it by what society claims can and can't be done. I've met many women who balance family, kids, and professional careers perfectly well.

John 16:33 says, *"I have told you these things, so that in me you may have peace. In this world you will have trouble. But take heart! I have overcome the world."* This scripture speaks about the trouble that the world inflicts upon us but how, by God's might, he overcame the world for us.

This is why I believe you can have it all. With enough MaxOut living and faith in God, I truly believe that you'll be able to "have it all" sooner than you think. If you never stop trying, you'll never stop succeeding.

Carpe Diem: Seize the Day

How many days in your life do you think you've fully seized and taken advantage of? Most people will say maybe one or two. And even then, they doubt that the days were properly seized. It's a strange human condition to not want to try our best at things.

We have this impulse to hold back, like we might run out of talent if we overuse it. This, of course, is ridiculous! You can't run out of talent or potential—these are infinite. So why don't you see more people seizing the day if there is nothing to lose?

Fear—I believe that we're afraid that, if we do leave it all out there, we'll discover that we aren't good enough. When you finally find your limits, it can be very damaging to your ego and to your self-esteem. A brilliant artist may be awful at landscapes even though he is excellent at all other forms of modern art.

Would you think more or less of the artist if they focused on landscapes and became better at painting them from hard work? I would say more because they're trying to strengthen their own weak points, which is a noble pursuit.

With this in mind—what imagined fears do people concoct to prevent them from living life to the fullest? Here is a list of some that you may recognize:

> ➤ I'm waiting for things to get better or waiting for the perfect time.
> ➤ There isn't enough time to make these things happen.
> ➤ I don't have enough money to make things happen.
> ➤ I'm not good enough, and it won't help.
> ➤ It's not going to change anything.

That last one is my favorite. It's the perfect representation of what a negative attitude can do to someone. Believing that nothing you can do in your life will change things is just ludicrous. Every action has a reaction. If you focus on doing the right things, you can change every single part of your life if you want to.

So here is your wake up call. Stop waiting for life to start; it started the day you were born. It's impossible to find the time to make things happen; you have to make it happen. If that means emptying your life of other things, then so be it. There are always ways around the "I have no time" excuse.

Say yes to life and to all the wondrous opportunities that come your way. A day not seized is a day wasted—that is your new mantra. MaxOut your potential by actively searching for new opportunities on a daily basis. There is no time like the present to enjoy life. Be there wholly, fully, and completely, and live in these moments like they are running out. Because they are!

Procrastination and Potential

Procrastination is the enemy of proactive people. For people brimming with potential, procrastination can do some serious damage and actually prevent them from ever discovering what they are made of. Yet it's an impulse we all share.

Remember the time you had to finish that bit of work at home and put it off until the very last second? Then, when you had to do it, you rushed to get it done. Life can be like that sometimes when you procrastinate about big life decisions. Sometimes you wait too long and then rush into the decision you make.

> ➤ Procrastinating forces you to put off things that you should be doing right now, which not only adds stress in your life but overloads and burns you out.
> ➤ People that procrastinate too often become lazy and find it increasingly difficult to motivate themselves to do anything worthwhile.
> ➤ Procrastination causes you to act out of stress, fear, and anxiety—which results in rushed work that could have been a lot better if you took your time with it.
> ➤ Procrastination is a powerful force that can turn you away from the action altogether. Not fixing the lawn mower, for example, will cause your garden to become overgrown. But because the mower is hard to fix, you put it off. Eventually, instead of fixing the mower, you buy a new one because it's easier.

- Getting extensions on work will only make you procrastinate even more and, once again, come down to the last second of the deadline.
- Procrastination is a bad trait to have as an employee, an employer, or a business owner. No one likes procrastinators because they are unreliable.
- Procrastination is easy to practice, which eventually becomes a habit. Soon you'll be leaving everything in life to the last minute because you think it's easier that way. The reality of the situation is that you've just made life much harder for yourself.

Your potential is only as great as your will to fight off procrastination whenever it decides to come knocking. It can be very difficult to plan to do things early, but they make all the difference in your life when you do. Being a "work first" kind of person makes you valuable and reliable—which is something people like.

Another benefit of getting things done early is that you have time to review them and make them even more powerful and brilliant. A work presentation, for example, could really benefit from your potential, not your procrastination.

I'm here to tell you that you can have it all, but you have to become a non-procrastinator first. There is just no way you'll succeed in this world if you continually put off your opportunities and choose to be last instead of proactive.

Listing Your Heart's Desires

It's no secret that people that manage to follow their heart's desires are usually the most successful. Not only do they become successful, but they achieve something that very few people ever get to achieve—fulfillment. When you reach for the desires of your heart, you don't stop working until you get them.

Ephesians 3:20 says, *"Now glory be to God! By His mighty power at work within me, He is able to accomplish infinitely more than I would ever dare to ask or hope for."* I believe that our potential helps guide us on our path in life. God works through us in mysterious ways!

It's also the reason that we are able to make the desires of our hearts manifest. Using our desire as a guide and our potential as mode of transport for getting there, we hastily rush towards an end goal instead of enjoying the path.

Once you desire something enough, it really does guide your actions. That's where the law of attraction comes from. You put out actions, and in return, you get positive responses from the universe. Take a moment now to list the desires of your heart:

- ➤ Consider that you are a product of your own reality. This is the truth of your life. What you desire can be acquired if you acknowledge how badly you want it.
- ➤ Find some abstract emotions to help you pinpoint what you really want from life: words like peace, joy, harmony, and wisdom. Now add some things to your list that resonate with these words.
- ➤ Making choices, good choices, is essential to finding out what your heart really wants. Bad decisions will only lead you away from truth and away from what you need to become a complete person.
- ➤ Wanting something projects it into the future. But it will remain "unmanifested" if you don't work on a plan to acquire your desires.

> Love is the most powerful energy in creation. If your heart's desire lacks love, then perhaps it not a desire so much as a "want." Learn to tell the difference between what you want and what you can't live without.
> Have faith that your heart's desires will be fulfilled if you work towards them each day. Even if it's in a small way, moving forward still gets you closer to the outcome.

For desires of the heart to become real, it will require dedication, commitment, and a proactive mentality. You can't sit by and hope that your desires will come true; rather, you have to go out and make them come true.

You have the power to "have it all"; you've always had it. When you create a list of your heart's desires, you'll begin to see how attainable they are with a bit of hard work.

How to Get From Want to Have

Getting from want to have is actually easier than you think. You see, when your goals are aligned with God's plan for your life, the true desires of your heart will be along a similar vein. The first step is realizing that you can actually make this dream of yours come true.

All it will take are a few steps in the right direction. Merely wanting something isn't enough; you have to really want it in order to put in the amount of work required to make it happen. For a struggling actress, this may mean moving to LA or Hollywood and finding an agent that can actually help her put together a good career.

The process will require clean, good decisions that are in line with your mantra—MaxOut your potential! How can you use your talents to help you get what you want faster? For the actress, it could mean putting together a highlights reel of her best screen moments. We often don't consider the sacrifices that we make for the things we really want in our lives.

And what we want sometimes isn't always good for us. If you pray about it and think about it often—and it will actively benefit your life—then it's worth pursuing. Wanting a new car, on the other hand, doesn't have any REAL life benefits because it's a material possession.

Yes, you can drive the car, but you could probably have bought a much cheaper one to get the same results. A desire of the heart is more to do with things you want to have HAPPEN to you in your life. To make them happen, you have to prepare for them.

The actress, for example, may have gone to acting school to improve her chances of being a good actress. She has starred in every advert and short film possible to gain experience. The leap of faith came when she moved—then the hardships really started.

But she stuck in there and worked very, very hard to secure roles in some minor films. She networked, made sure she was a delight to work with, and soon she landed her first real movie role. Suddenly this actress from acting school was living her heart's desire—to be a real actress in a motion picture.

Begin by accurately identifying what you want and the obstacles that may prevent you from acquiring it. You can put this down in a two-column format. How will you overcome these obstacles? Write it down. What needs to happen on a micro scale in order for your heart's desires to come true?

Then create your magnificent plan of action. Step by step, detail as best you can how you will transform your want into a have. Then put that plan of action into effect. Formulate a timeline and work every day on your plan until you inch closer to your goal. That's how you make things happen in the real world!

Positive Reinforcement

Positive reinforcement is used when a decision needs to be made but you're having doubts about it. In fact, positive reinforcement is deeply entwined with the decision-making process. It involves adding a reinforcing stimulus to your behavior so that this behavior is more likely to occur again.

When you've managed to achieve something truly special, that's when you need positive reinforcement the most. Here's the trick! It should come from inside you as well. While positive things are always nice from other people, they need to be expressed by you as well. This is because motivation is a key ingredient in maxing out your potential.

Psalm 18:2 says, *"The LORD is my rock and my fortress and my deliverer, my God, my rock, in whom I take refuge; my shield and the horn of my salvation, my stronghold."* I love this scripture because it speaks about the strength we can all find in the Lord, no matter how urgently we need it or desperately want it.

It's important to get into the habit of recognizing when you do positive things in your life so that you can repeat them—and stay on your destined path. If you allow big moments of achievement to go by without any internal fanfare, you may feel let down.

Sometimes people will decide that it was just too much hard work the first time and that the reward wasn't enough to compensate them for their effort. But how can you put a price on living life to the fullest? How can you calculate what achieving one of your heart's true desires will be? There is simply no way to do that. This is why you need to be prepared to give YOURSELF positive reinforcement when it's necessary. Reflect carefully on your journey when you reach a big milestone and allow yourself to become emotional and to really feel the impact of the change in your life.

> Use natural reinforcers and be open to celebrating your success. Half the fun is learning to enjoy it when we succeed. Don't forget to feel good about yourself, to congratulate yourself, and to even reward yourself for doing something positive.
> Social reinforcers will happen when other people in your life experience your success. They will congratulate you and compliment you on a job well done.
> Tangible reinforcers involve some kind of physical reward. I've always been big on buying myself ice-cream if my day happens to go extremely well. These little motivators will get you through the day and ready to meet the next one.

Treat yourself the moment your success is achieved—don't wait. Positive reinforcement works best when the moment and the rewards are enjoyed close together. Think of your last birthday and how you enjoyed presents on that day. Presents a week later from your relative overseas didn't make you feel very special because the time gap was too vast.

09

How To Max Out Your Potential

"The potential of the average person is like a huge ocean unsailed, a new continent unexplored, a world of possibilities waiting to be released and channeled toward some great good."

BRIAN TRACY

I learned a long time ago that to realize your true potential in this life means that you'll have to swim against the stream. Daring to be different is the missing ingredient in the MaxOut formula. You already know that not many people are able to live life to the fullest, and that gives you the edge on them.

But it also makes you different from them. Don't be afraid of the changes that will happen in your life. People close to you may have doubts, fears, and opinions—but it boils down to two things: Do you believe enough in yourself to make it all a reality; and do you believe that God will guide you and be with you the entire time? If you do, you're ready!

Turning Potential into Reality

To turn potential into reality is going to require a few things. These things you must be prepared for, in order to thrive under this new life mantra. MaxOut your potential to achieve all that life has to offer. Here's how:

> ➤ *Time dedication.* You will need a lot of time to develop who you are and where you want to go in life. Set aside time to work on yourself, to inch closer to your dreams, to put plans into action—and to take advantage of the best opportunities.
> ➤ *Unlearn what you think you know about your destiny.* No one but God really knows where our life paths will take us. Following yours will be exciting, scary, thrilling, and exhilarating. Don't peg yourself as one specific thing. Be open to all new ideas.
> ➤ *Forget what you know about talent and potential.* Yours is unlimited, which means without end. Never

stop learning how you can develop your talent and transform that potential of yours into new creations, ideas, and innovations for the world.
- *Be sensitive of your own feelings.* This will be an emotional rollercoaster, and not everyone will be on board. Be prepared to stand proud and true and to support your decision to live a MaxOut life.
- *Appreciate everything, and collect your moments wisely.* Life is made up of exquisite moments that come and go every day. Don't forget to appreciate the moments you are able to create because of your unlimited potential.

No matter what obstacles you'll face, remember to aim high. The higher you aim the sweeter it will be when you finally achieve your goals and fulfill your potential. Turning potential into reality can take years depending on the goal you have to reach. As long as you never give up, you will never fail.

The Scarier Reality

I'm going to use a scare tactic called "reality." People don't usually talk about it because it can be really depressing. But these are the facts. Right now your life isn't going so well. You aren't happy in your job, and your home life could use a lot of work.

Depending on your situation, if you don't make the commitment to change today—to embrace the MaxOut your potential program—you could end up where you are 30 years from now. Only now, you've spent your entire life on misery, struggle, and being wholly unremarkable.

No one wants to fade into the shadows of this world. We all want recognition for what we're good at; we all want to make a difference. It's a scary reality when you consider the facts. Most people won't make a difference at all. They will continue living their average lives and being unhappy—because they never found the courage to break free from it.

1 Peter 4:10 says, *"Each one should use whatever gift he has received to serve others, faithfully administering God's grace in its various forms."* I believe that the world would be a much better place if everyone was able to reach their true potential. There would be no more unhappiness, struggle, or pain.

People would feel adequate, so there would be less war and fighting in the world. The sense of peace and belonging that comes with walking along your destined path is paramount to leading a happy life. If you don't know your purpose in this world, you'll never feel like a real part of it.

Modern technology tries to connect us together but tears us more apart. We fight battles in our working lives and lose. People ignore us. We get treated badly. Kids get into trouble. Marriages fall on hard times. Money dries up.

I know better than anyone how hard this will be for you. But the alternative is even more terrifying. I don't want you to have had this opportunity only to let it fall on rocky ground and never take root. I don't want you to miss out on what life can be if you only decide to seize it. No one can make these decisions for you.

Life doesn't have to be this hard! "It's not that bad" isn't good enough. I want you to wake up every morning and revel in the happiness that you've managed to bring to yourself because you're following your destined path.

The reality is that, if you ignore this opportunity, you might never change. You'll continue working in your horrible job and struggling with life. You'll devalue who you are and never really discover what you're made of. That's no life to lead.

I want you to embrace this opportunity now. "I will MaxOut my potential every day!" Make this pledge to yourself and hold yourself to it. Ask yourself the question—what have I done for my potential today? If the answer is nothing, then realign your goals!

MaxOut to Win It All

Life is not something that happens to us as we passively stand around eating, sleeping, and earning money. It's something that needs to be embraced—that needs to be won! If you're going to win it all in this crazy game of life, then you have to use ALL the tools that God gave you. That means whipping out your potential whenever you can.

Once you've settled on the idea that you will be living life to the MAX from now on, you begin to see things differently. There are an insurmountable amount of things that you could achieve if you put your mind to it. One person really could change the world.

The most inspirational, incredible people that have affected our literature, society, and ethics have done so because they decided to follow their life path all the way to the end. They woke up every morning eager to try new things and experience something different.

How often do you experience something different? You can't hide away from it anymore! Different is good. If you don't test yourself, you'll never discover who you really are. It's your responsibility, as someone who wants it all from life, to find out what they have to offer.

Romans 5:5 says, *"And hope does not put us to shame, because God's love has been poured into our hearts through the Holy Spirit who has been given to us." I hope that whoever I turn out to be in 10–20 years will be the kind of person who leaves a legacy in this world. I've always wanted to help people—that is my calling.*

In order for me to succeed, you have to succeed! Those are the rules. But get this: Life is a race to the finish line. None of us know how much time we have left on this earth. What we do know is that making it here on earth is hard. You have to play to win if you're going to be a serious contender.

Most people don't play to win in life. They might as well be plants or lamps for all they do in their day. But this, like everything, is a choice. You can choose to be a serious player right now. You can stand up and say, "No! I won't let life get the better of me; I'll get the better of life!" It begins with the one weapon you have—your talent.

Once you begin to move forward and make things happen, no one will be able to stop you. Momentum is a magical thing. Your first real success will come, and then more—until you are far above the place you thought you'd be. That's the great thing about potential; it lifts you higher than your dreams can take you.

Living by Example

I spoke briefly earlier about wishing that everyone in the world could live life to the max. The only way to make sure that this happens is by affecting your life. You, in turn, can be the light that shines on others and spreads the word. You see, I believe that you can LIVE by example and teach others to do the same just by watching you do it.

The old saying "lead by example" refers to teaching people what the right and wrong way is by showing them how you approach the situation. Living by example is similar except you will prove to people through your achievements, success, and happiness that living life to the max is the right thing to do.

Living by example means that you need to be aware that people are watching you and judging you for your actions each day. If you can actively inspire these people to ask what your secret is, then you've won! Just another way you can win in this life.

After all, winning is about affecting other people. Everything we do for our own benefit is designed to help others in some way, shape, or form. It's the way God designed us. An artist contributes to the beauty of the world, a dentist to innovations in human dentistry.

We all have our niches where we can make the most impact. Your colleagues and friends need to notice that there has been a change in you. You need to grab life with both hands and hang on. Others need to experience why you're doing that!

Yours kids, for example, will learn how to live their lives by following your example. If you're the kind of person that doesn't take risks—that is consumed by fear and that never amounts to much—your kids may turn out the same way. You don't want that! We always want more for our kids than we had ourselves.

Living by example means that your kids will see how courageous, strong, and brimming with faith you are. They will carry these lessons into life with them and, in turn, make a positive impact on the people they meet. It's a cycle that needs to be started and never stopped.

Maxing out your potential is about so much more than reaching for a dream or improving your life. It's about the core of who you are and what you're capable of doing—and believe me, you were born to influence others.

The mere fact that you are reading this book tells me that you want more from life. This is your chance to take it! Say goodbye to your negative thinking processes, unfulfilled life, and perpetual struggle. Say hello to happiness, greatness, and the chance to make a real difference in the world.

Inspiration and Motivation to MaxOut

Before I go to sleep every night, I have a MaxOut ritual that I go through. I think about what I achieved that day and congratulate myself for doing a good job. I then think about the little obstacles that cropped up and how I dealt with them.

I go over in my mind whether I could have done better or not. I consciously make the decision to be even better tomorrow. I check my schedule, I say a prayer, and I go to bed. This is my evening ritual. When I wake up in the morning, I feel fully motivated to fulfill the promise I made to myself and to God before bed last night.

2 Corinthians 4:16 says, *"So we do not lose heart. Though our outer self is wasting away, our inner self is being renewed day by day."* God has the ability to renew our minds, bodies, and spirits. If you ever find yourself waning, or unable to MaxOut your day, remember that spending some time with God is all that is required.

Here are a few other things I like to do if I'm not feeling motivated enough:

- *Watch the sun rise and marvel at God's glory.* I like to do this with a hot cup of coffee on my own in the mornings.
- *Spend some time outdoors or with nature.* There's nothing like natural bird or wildlife to remind you how important life is and how fleeting it is as well.
- *Read self-help books and literature,* not only to improve myself, but to develop my skills as someone who helps other people. Inspirational words can go a long way to motivating you for the day.
- *Do something selfless for a stranger or someone in need.* There's no better way to feel good about your life than to help someone that needs help.
- *Acknowledge the people in your life that make it worth living.* Remind yourself that your achievements become their achievements and that you all succeed together.
- *Do something completely new.* Whether it's riding a horse for the first time or eating at a new restaurant, you'll be surprised how one new experience can motivate you to do better in your life.
- *Listen to inspiring music that speaks to your soul.* You don't have to do it all the time, but when you're feeling especially depleted, a good song can really pick you up.

Watching my kids play in the yard is also an inexplicable source of inspiration for me; perhaps you'll feel the same about your kids. It's important to stay motivated to keep up the motivation for your MaxOut life, or you could slip back into old habits.

Your Life, Your Rules

This is your life, and these are your rules. Though, now that you've decided to MaxOut your potential every day, there will be a bunch of new rules that you'll have to consider. These rules are meant to help you as much as possible, so pay attention!

1. If I'm not living life to the max, I'm missing out on my opportunity to be the best that I can be. I won't let that happen!
2. Do what you love to do, and do it as often as you can. Make a plan to be the person that loves their work and works because they love it.
3. If anything in your life crops up that you don't like, change it. Nothing in life is written in stone—you have the power to change everything.
4. You are more than one job or one thing. You can be many things and still find yourself reaching greater heights as you MaxOut your potential.
5. Watching TV series, movies, and documentaries is fun, but it wastes a lot of your time. If you find yourself short on time, then cut back on these "time wasters."
6. If you still haven't found your soul mate, stop looking for them. They will appear when you're solidly back on your life path.
7. Appreciate the food you put into your body. It gives you the energy you need to be extraordinary and take everything you want from life.

8. Life can be simple if you know what your purpose is. This is because you have found your place in the world and can finally reach for the stars from your chosen platform.
9. Never stop learning, developing, changing, and evolving. Open your mind to new things and make the most of opportunities as they arise.
10. When the opportunity presents itself, share with others how you came to be on your life path, and inspire them to do the same.
11. Sometimes opportunities only happen once or twice. Make sure that you are seizing all opportunities so that you are getting the most out of life.
12. Take holidays and travel to new places. You can discover a lot about yourself when you're in a completely new area with no familiar surroundings.
13. Never stop creating. You were born a creator, and that's what you were meant to do. Apply it in your own life and to your work.
14. Life is about the people you come into contact with. Cherish them, connect with them, and influence them to be better people.
15. Never give up on your dreams, and wear your passion on your sleeve.

[10]

Six Lessons in Personal Growth

"If you don't go after what you want, you could spend your entire life settling for what you can get."

MO STEGALL

Aren't you tired of making excuses about who you are? I reached that point some years ago, when I was working for a large pharmaceutical company. I was great at my job, but I just wasn't happy with the way my life turned out. Then I learned these six lessons in personal growth, and I began decontaminating my soul and my life, one step at a time.

#1: The Positive Approach

From the moment you are born, you begin to learn about life. As you get older, you discover who you are and what you can do as a person. You learn relentlessly—until you hit the job market. Instead of continuing your journey of self-discovery, you begin to realize the way "the real world works" and that things are going to be perpetually hard from now on.

That's when we lose our positive approach to life and doors begin to close for us. You need to re-establish this positive approach to life so that possibility and freedom are invited back into your heart. It's never too late for you to evolve and become a person that lives life to the fullest, every moment of every day.

Who would you rather be—the office drone that lives for the weekend and then can't even enjoy it because they have no money? Or the dynamic person that steps into your life and inspires you because they can? All happy people are inspiring and seek to share their positive approach with the world.

It's only positive energy that can be put to good use for making your dreams come true. Negative energy pushes away positive change in your life. You need to rid yourself of it forever. I can't stress enough how important it is to approach life with this new positive mindset.

- ➤ You must be positive about the people you are around.
- ➤ You mustn't meet negativity with negativity, even if you're provoked.
- ➤ Go the extra mile—for yourself and for the people you love.
- ➤ Have a heart of forgiveness, and don't carry around grudges.
- ➤ Try and bless people in your life by doing something nice for them.
- ➤ Try to influence other people to be positive with your positivity.
- ➤ Be positive about experiences, and try to see the good in them.
- ➤ Turn problems into challenges with your positive attitude.
- ➤ Practice positive affirmations when you get the chance.

Like anything worth doing in life, changing from a negative to a positive mindset will take time and effort. But you should be able to experience the difference very soon after you begin. People will respond to you differently, and your life will begin to change.

#2: Attacking the Problem

Believe me when I say the number of obstacles that you're able to overcome in your life is directly related to the amount of success that you'll experience. That's why the second lesson you need to learn in order to live a MaxOut life is how to attack and solve problems.

You literally have to adopt the mindset of an attack dog for this. Allowing problems to linger only makes them worse. When they step into your courtyard, you need to attack them! And there's a good reason for that as well. Problems never stop coming at you in life, and they can pile up. Procrastination is the enemy of success.

That's why any problem that crops up needs to have a red painted bull's eye on its back. Learn to identify problems quickly so that you can solve them fast. A week before Christmas a few years ago, I had a problem with one of my clients, who was very upset over something that had happened during one of our sessions.

Instead of dealing with it, I took the time off to be with my family, believing that it would all blow over. When I got back to the office in the New Year, all of my clients were talking about the incident. That man had attended a Christmas networking event and had spread not-so-nice things about me to people, and word got around.

In this instance, I had done nothing wrong, but because I did not solve the problem when it arose, my business took a knock financially. You have to be careful of problems arising that get worse over time. Obstacles in life either come slowly or they happen very quickly, at the worst possible times. You need to be ready to deal with them whenever they arise.

Proverbs 23:7 says, *"As a man thinks in his heart, so is he."* Start thinking of yourself as a problem solver, and develop these skills. With all the adversity and chaos in our lives, it's incredible that more people don't develop valuable, problem-solving life skills.

> ▶ Examine what the problem is and why it is affecting your life.

- Accept that there is a problem, and acknowledge that it exists.
- Spend most of your time thinking about solutions.
- If you can't think of any viable solutions, ask for help.
- Break the problem down into manageable pieces.
- Learn something from the problem, and try not to repeat it.

This "attack dog" mentality that keeps you solving problems like a pro is an invaluable skill that you can use to get ahead. Never let problems get you down; there are always ways to overcome them, even if they seem impractical and impossible. God never gives you more than you can handle.

To truly MaxOut your potential, look deep within yourself and discover the lean, mean, problem-solving machine that's always been inside you!

#3: Moving Forward All the Time

The third greatest lesson I can teach you is to never stop moving forward with your life. There are a few things you should never stop doing, actually. Hopefully, this book has taught you the most important one—personal development. We are all on an incredible journey that is influenced by the decisions and choices that we make.

Unfortunately, most people are influenced by society and their own circumstances to make the WRONG decisions. They settle for what life gives them instead of taking what they want from life. This isn't moving forward; this is staying stagnant. It's positively the worst thing you can do if you're looking for a life of purpose and happiness.

I don't believe that God intended for us to live in a groundhog-like world, where everything is hard, boring, and repetitive. These are patterns of behavior that we choose to indulge in when we become disappointed or disillusioned with our lives. You just can't afford not to spend every waking moment working towards becoming the real you.

How will you know what you're made of if you don't get out there and experience life? Stop being a spectator in your own life! Do something unexpected and move forward. Sometimes, in order to move forward emotionally, you need to step back. That's why this book is filled with rarely uttered truths about the way you've chosen to live your life.

You stopped. Your career stopped. There was nothing to look forward to anymore because you gave up on yourself. You were never meant to do that. The good news is that moving forward just means placing one foot after the other again. Theoretically, it means planning, preparing, and taking action so that you can live your ideal life.

Your maximum potential is waiting to be unleashed on this world. And you won't believe how great it feels to finally get the recognition you deserve for being someone worth noticing. Positive, happy people that love what they do are always moving forward in some way. They try new things in their never ending quest for self-improvement.

That's how you should be. You've finally heard the truth, and the writing is on the wall. Your life isn't going to change until you get up and change it. I like to start with a list. I list all the things I need to change in my life first, and then I put a plan of action in place. Being proactive about how you feel every day is essential to being happy!

I charge you with this new way of living. Move forward in your career, never stop. Move forward in your marriage, never stop. Move forward in your social life, never stop. And above all, never stop taking all that life has to offer so that you can discover who you are in this world. You deserve a life on the move.

#4: Never Give Up

Lesson four is a tough one because there will be moments in your future when you're tempted to throw in the towel and give up. There is only one difference between a loser and a winner. The loser will always give up. If you want to win in life, then you need to become the epitome of perseverance.

It's not enough to lead your "average" life; that's not why you were put here. You were put on this earth to make an impact on people with your unique talents and potential. So, you may be tempted to give up because you have "enough" or because you've lost confidence in yourself—but don't.

We were given the ability to keep going—to overcome and to walk by faith—because not giving up is so important. 2 Chronicles 15:7 says, *"But you, take courage! Do not let your hands be weak, for your work shall be rewarded."* Even though tough times will come around, and quitting seems like the right thing to do, if you stick it out, you will be rewarded.

I grew up in the same society you did. I know about the temptations and how our modern culture promotes inactivity and demands immediate results. It's what makes it so difficult to hang in there for a while, to achieve something really worthwhile. But once you do—and you've been through the hard work and dedication—it's twice as worth it.

Make a pledge to yourself right now that you won't give up on your ideal life. You can tap into that incredible potential of yours and make anything happen. You are a powerful individual who has been blessed with talents, gifts, and the ability to make your own dreams come true! Now, that is something to hold out for.

Believe in yourself and you can make miracles happen. Don't forget that the fact that you are even alive is a miracle. Not giving up means that you'll need to work on your faith, motivation, and dedication skills.

If you find yourself waning, renew your faith in God. There are success stories all over the world if you need to read them; stories about how people overcame impossible odds to find a successful life of happiness and fulfillment. If they can do it with their problems, you can as well. There's no difference, except they never, ever gave up.

Keep this book next to your bed, and re-read it when you're looking for some inspiration. Everyone needs to push through the hardships sometimes, tough as they may be. All you can do is trust in yourself, in the Lord, and in the path you've taken.

#5: Knowing Your Limits Are Few

When you add a newfound will to succeed to self-belief and faith in God, magical things tend to happen. After a while, as your faith grows, you begin to realize that you don't actually have many limits holding you back in life. Most limits are self-imposed, and they cause damage because they impact the perception we have of ourselves.

I'll never forget when I realized I could do anything, be anything. If I wanted to go to medical school, I could do that. If I wanted to be a lawyer, veterinarian, or scuba diving shark tank instructor, I could learn how, and that would be my new life. Lesson number five is concerned with recognizing that your potential is far greater than you imagined.

I've been many things in my life with great success. I guess that should have been the clue that I was looking for when I realized my life was in turmoil. But realization of my potential only came much later, when I stopped trying to be one thing. If my goal in life was to be inspirational, I could be many things.

Today I'm a life coach, a corporate trainer, an entrepreneur, a guest blogger, an inspirational speaker, a retreat leader and keynote speaker, and now an author. All of these avenues I've expanded into because I had the potential to share my gifts with the world in different ways. So, don't back yourself into a corner.

The reality is that you have very few limits. Even a humble carpenter can become incredibly famous these days with the online media being so well developed. The sky is the limit on your earning potential and on your abilities. As long as you continue to be better—to improve yourself and your life—you will never face limits you can't overcome.

That's why you have to make MaxOut your way of life. Being all you can be is so much more than you initially think. It gives you that self-esteem you've always needed; it validates your place in this world and why you were born into it. It helps you connect to others as you share your work passion with the world.

If I can leave you with a piece of advice, it would be this—the only limits you face are created in your mind. It will always be your job to break through these limits and to explore the adventure that comes afterwards. This is how you'll learn and grow and become a significant person, who is not only happy but living life to its fullest every moment of the day.

When you start using this advice in your own life, remember that limits are no more than opportunities. You can either choose to strengthen them or change them for the better. Whatever you decide, keep in mind that an unlimited person in a limited world can effect positive change in a really meaningful way.

#6: Getting the Most from Life

MaxOut has been about learning the truths and skills you need to get the most out of your life. When you approach life knowing that you are able to overcome any obstacle, it becomes easier to express your potential in creative ways.

The average lifespan may be 77 years, but that's only 28,105 days. For some of us, it will be longer; for some—a lot shorter. None of us know when we'll be joining our Father in heaven. What we do know is this. God made you a certain way. He placed you on this earth to do something with what he gave you.

1 John 5:14–15 says, *"And this is our confidence, that if we pray according to His will, He will hear us, and give us what we ask for, because our desires are in agreement with His thoughts for us."* When you align your goals with your destined path, incredible things happen—I've seen it.

I honestly don't believe that we are supposed to allow life to do whatever it wants to us. That was never the deal. Yet thanks to our increasingly passive society, we become like sheep. We do what we are told. And we are told to be content with an unfulfilled life. That's never going to work out!

Enough being passive! It's time to switch to an active life of going out and being all you can be. Even if all you can be is your town's best baker, then that's something all your own. We all deserve to find our place in this world, yet we are so tuned out. We let decades go by as we suffer in misery because we have ignored the pursuit of truth and happiness.

You have an infinite amount of potential that fuels your talent and makes you great. Everyone has something special, something that sets them apart from other people. It's your job, your duty, to explore this talent by using your potential every day until your last breath!

Don't make the horrible mistake of closing this book and never changing your life. Regret is not something that can replace the benefits of getting the most from life. We've reached the end, which makes me sad for two reasons. I know that some of you will try to change and fail because it's just too hard. Others will really shake things up in their lives.

Whatever you choose to do, remember this—if you aren't finding moments of joy throughout your day, then that day is wasted. Learning, growing, evolving, and expanding your potential is a never ending pursuit of those joyous moments that make it all worth it.

Go, get the most from life, and do it while this information is still fresh in your mind. This is one of those opportunities that rarely come around, when you have the chance to start over and be who you want to be.

Conclusion

Hopefully, you've learned some new things about yourself and have come to the realization that you are responsible for your own life. I've spoken at many seminars where people have come up to me and commented on the life-changing speech I gave them for 60 minutes.

I don't know why, but this information always reaches some people more than others. Perhaps for it to strike home, you have to be totally honest with yourself—and not many people are willing to do that.

I just want you to know that you CAN and MUST live a life where you get to MaxOut your potential. Not only will you be blessing the world with your God-given talents, but you'll inspire others to do the same. Imagine if everyone in the world found out who they were and were able to lead their ideal lives.

Be strong and courageous in pursuit of your dreams, and never give up on them. Be open to change, be positive about your experiences, and never let any obstacles stand in your destined path. This is the best advice that I can give you for what is to come.

I'm still on my journey and discovering new things about my potential all the time. A few years ago I would never have stood up in front of people and been able to hold the attention of hundreds of people at a time. Today I do it like an old pro!

You can choose to be the hero in your life story. But heroes go through a journey of self-discovery. They push themselves and test their skills. They are often tempted and pulled off the path, but they quickly find their way back again. You need to be like a superhero.

Deep down, you've always felt like there was something special waiting to be released into the world—admit it! God gives each of us something we can call our own. You do nothing but praise God when you take the time to use the potential he gave you.

Don't walk away from this opportunity again. There are only so many days left in your life. It's time to make those changes, to brave those storms, and to come out on the other side better than ever before. That is your destiny, my friend.

It's time to MaxOut your potential!

-Zenovia Andrews

References

Chapter 1

Ali, Muhammad Quotes, Brainyquote, http://www.brainyquote.com/quotes/authors/m/muhammad_ali.html

Munoz, Belinda, *7 Reasons Why Failing Is Better Than Quitting*, http://thehalfwaypoint.net/2009/09/7-reasons-why-failing-is-better-than-quitting/

Sabol, Dave, *The Difference Between Failing and Quitting*, http://www.davesabol.com/blog/2012/01/the-difference-between-failing-and-quitting/

Kipko, Bogdan, *Five Reliable Reasons Why You Should Not Quit or Give Up*, http://bogdankipko.com/five-reliable-reasons-why-you-should-not-quit-or-give-up

Blum, Deborah, *Finding Strength: How to Overcome Anything*, http://www.psychologytoday.com/articles/199805/finding-strength-how-overcome-anything

The Original Poem, The Don't Quit Poem, http://www.thedontquitpoem.com/thePoem.htm

Blackson, Kute, *Don't Give Up on Your Dreams*, http://thedailylove.com/dont-give-up-on-your-dreams/

Why Should Never Give Up on Your Dreams, http://www.purposefairy.com/1830/why-give-up-on-your-dreams/

Newman, Leigh, *How to Pursue Your Dreams: Goals You Can Never Give Up On,* http://www.huffingtonpost.com/2012/10/05/how-to-pursue-your-dreams-impossible-goals_n_1926915.html

Chapter 2

Twain, Mark Quotes, Thinkexist.com, http://thinkexist.com/quotation/twenty_years_from_now_you_will_be_more/215220.html

5 Elements of an Effective Decision Making Process, Sources of Insight, http://sourcesofinsight.com/5-elements-of-an-effective-decision-making-process/

The Decision Making Process: 7 Strategies For Success, http://www.lifecompassblog.com/the-decision-making-process-7-strategies-for-success/

Taking Action, 40 Bible Verses About, http://www.openbible.info/topics/taking_action

Patt, *The Reason Self-Improvement Is Important,* http://personaldevelopmentchallenges.com/the-reason-self-improvement-is-important/

Cranford, Janet, *Is Career Happiness Really Possible?* http://www.careerchangepathways.com/career-happiness/

Porter, Bethany, *Improve Family Time,* http://parenting.slides.kaboose.com/328-improve-your-family-time

Haas, Rebekah, *How to Improve Family Relationships,* http://voices.yahoo.com/how-improve-family-relationships-208567.html?cat=7

Gentleness, 61 Bible Verses About, http://www.openbible. info/topics/gentleness

Matta, Christy, *Improve Your Emotional and Spiritual Well-Being: 8 Easy, Everyday Tips,* http://blogs.psychcentral. com/dbt/2012/03/improve-your-emotional-and-spiritual-well-being-8-easy-everyday-tips/

Chapter 3

Maxwell, John C, Goodreads, http://www.goodreads.com/ quotes/361608-if-you-don-t-have-peace-it-isn-t-because-someone

Hall, Susan, *Get Ahead by Putting Your Talents on a Different Stage,* http://www.itbusinessedge.com/cm/blogs/hall/get-ahead-by-putting-your-talents-on-a-different-stage/?cs=46711

Talent, 12 Bible Verses About, http://www.openbible.info/ topics/talent

Warren, Rick, *Make the Most of Your Talents,* http:// purposedriven.com/blogs/dailyhope/index.html?contentid=7383

Marston, Ralph, *Five Ways You Can Empower Yourself to Achieve,* http://greatday.com/nmot/features/five-ways-you-can-empower-yourself-to-achieve.html

DeMaio, James, *Questions That Will Help You Understand Yourself and Others Better,* http://nerdfighters.ning.com/ group/christiannerdfighters/forum/topics/on-truth-knowledge-and-faith?xg_source=activity

Madhok, James, *Questions That Will Help You Understand Yourself,* http://www.healthguidance.org/entry/12758/1/Questions-That-Will-Help-You-Understand-Yourself.html

Chapter 4

Quotes About Positive Thinking, Goodreads.com, http://www.goodreads.com/quotes/tag/positive-thinking

Positive Thinking, 68 Bible Verses About, http://www.openbible.info/topics/positive_thinking

Making Mistakes, 24 Bible Verses About, http://www.openbible.info/topics/making_mistakes

Uy, Michelle, *10 Tips to Overcome Negative Thoughts: Positive Thinking Made Easy,* http://tinybuddha.com/blog/10-tips-to-overcome-negative-thoughts-positive-thinking-made-easy/

Chopra, Deepak, *Ask Deepak: How to Be a Positive Thinker,* http://www.oprah.com/spirit/How-to-Be-a-Positive-Thinker-Ask-Deepak

Griswold, Jeff, *How to Become a Positive Thinker,* http://www.trans4mind.com/counterpoint/index-success-abundance/griswold2.shtml

Sasson, Remez, *The Power of Positive Thinking,* http://www.successconsciousness.com/index_000009.htm

Wiseman, Richard, *Self Help: Forget Positive Thinking, Try Positive Action,* http://www.guardian.co.uk/science/2012/jun/30/self-help-positive-thinking

Example Affirmations, http://www.vitalaffirmations.com/affirmations.htm#example affirmations

Positive Thinking Positive Affirmations, http://www.freeaffirmations.org/positive-thinking-positive-affirmations

FinerMinds Team, *Change Your Mind With Positive Thinking Affirmations*, http://www.finerminds.com/mind-power/positive-thinking-affirmations/

Chapter 5

Courage Quotes, BrainyQuote, http://www.brainyquote.com/quotes/keywords/courage.html

David, *Bible Verses About Courage: 20 Great Scripture Quotes*, http://www.whatchristianswanttoknow.com/bible-verses-about-courage-20-great-scripture-quotes/

Wiley, Josh, *Bible Verses About Boldness: 10 Courageous Scriptures*, http://voices.yahoo.com/bible-verses-boldness-10-courageous-scriptures-7680522.html

Williams, Pamela, *Bible Verses About Faith: 20 Popular Scripture Quotes*, http://www.whatchristianswanttoknow.com/bible-verses-about-faith-20-popular-scripture-quotes/

Ni, Preston, *How to Find Your Best Career and Get Paid Doing What You Love*, http://www.psychologytoday.com/blog/communication-success/201205/how-find-your-best-career-get-paid-doing-what-you-love

A Leap of Faith Begins by Choosing to Follow Your Heart, http://www.choosing-life-my-way.com/leap-of-faith.html

MacIntyre, Scott, *The Leap of Faith: Why Taking Risks Can Be Worth It*, http://www.pickthebrain.com/blog/the-leap-of-faith-why-taking-risks-can-be-worth-it/

Faith Is Fundamental to Success, http://www.peakgenius.com/faithisfundamentaltosuccess.html

Power of Faith, http://www.success-attitude.com/principles/faith.html

15 Dynamic Principles To Make Your Dreams Come True, http://www.internetworldstats.com/articles/art010.htm

Chapter 6

Marati, Jessica, *30 Quotes on Overcoming Challenges*, http://ecosalon.com/30-quotes-on-overcoming-challenges/

Mahoney, Kelli, *Sunday Scripture: Ephesians 3:20*, http://christianteens.about.com/b/2010/01/17/sunday-scripture-ephesians-320.htm

Overcoming Adversity, http://www.buzzle.com/articles/overcoming-adversity.html

Debate and Relate, http://www.debateandrelate.com/showthread.php?t=2873

Jordan, Rebecca, *Five Simple Steps to Discover God's Plan for You*, http://www.rebeccabarlowjordan.com/five-simple-steps-to-discover-gods-plans-for-you/

What Empowers You, http://www.worldwidehealth.com/health-article-What-Empowers-You.html

Bininger, Angela, *What Empowers You?* http://angelabininger.com/2010/02/03/256/

What Fills You and What Drains You, http://kevinmartineau.ca/what-fills-you-and-what-drains-you/

Top Ten Tips to Overcome Obstacles to Success, http://mysuperchargedlife.com/blog/ten-top-tips-to-overcome-obstacles-to-success/

Margolies, Lynn, *How to Overcome Obstacles to Positive Change,* http://psychcentral.com/lib/2012/how-to-overcome-obstacles-to-positive-change/all/1/

Chapter 7

Fear Quotes, BrainyQuote, http://www.brainyquote.com/quotes/keywords/fear.html

Smith, Christine, *50 Scriptures Verses on Fear,* http://www.womensbiblecafe.com/2011/05/50-scripture-verses-on-fear/

Fear Bible Verses, Bibestudytools.com, http://www.biblestudytools.com/topical-verses/fear-bible-verses/

Brenner, Gail, *10 Life-Changing Facts About Fear: Take Two,* http://aflourishinglife.com/2012/01/facts-about-fear-2/

Why Your Fears Are Killing Your Dreams, http://undergroundsuccess.com/382/why-your-fears-are-killing-your-dreams/

Fear Kills Your Creativity, http://nisharaghavan.com/fear-kills-your-creativity/

Roth, JD, *How To Build Confidence and Destroy Fear,* http://www.getrichslowly.org/blog/2009/02/17/how-to-build-confidence-and-destroy-fear/

Joel, *5 Ways to Destroy The Illusion of Fear,* http://addicted2success.com/success-advice/5-ways-to-destroy-the-illusion-of-fear/

Christine, *The Secret to Destroying Fear,* http://riverofthoughts.com/writing/the-secret-to-destroying-fear/

Campbell, Polly, *How to Cultivate the Courage to Deal With Daily Challenges,* http://life.gaiam.com/article/how-cultivate-courage-deal-daily-challenges

Chapter 8

Quotes of Confidence, http://thisnewlifeofmind.blogspot.com/2010/04/quotes-of-confidence.html

http://succeedasyourownboss.com/01/2010/10-bible-verses-every-small-business-owner-needs/

Scriptures on Success, http://www.fjfj.cc/declarations/ScripturesonSuccess.pdf

Being Positive, 85 Bible Verse About, http://www.openbible.info/topics/being_positive

Ten Tried and True Steps to Realize Your Heart's Desires, http://www.fernstewartwelch.com/content.php?info_id=22

Tan, Enoch, *You Can Always Get What Your Heart Desires Most,* http://www.mindreality.com/you-can-always-get-what-your-heart-desires-most

Why Procrastination Is BAD for You, and Even Worse for Those Who Love You, http://jesserice.com/2012/05/why-procrastination-is-bad-for-you-and-even-worse-for-those-who-love-you/

10 Reasons Why Procrastination Is Bad, http://gmadventure2010.blogspot.com/2010/03/10-reasons-why-procrastination-is-bad.html

10 Ways to Seize the Day, http://sharonmarshall.wordpress.com/2009/05/26/10-ways-to-seize-the-day/

Thum, Myrko, *Carpe Diem – How to Seize the Day,* http://www.myrkothum.com/carpe-diem-how-to-seize-the-day/

Rizvi, Jamila, *What's Wrong With Wanting to Have It All?* http://www.mamamia.com.au/social/having-it-all/

Cherry, Kendra, *What Is Positive Reinforcement,* http://psychology.about.com/od/operantconditioning/f/positive-reinforcement.htm

The Seven Steps to Manifesting, http://www.dreamsalive.com/7stepsmanifst.html

Chapter 9

Quotes About Potential, Goodreads, http://www.goodreads.com/quotes/tag/potential

Josh, *Bible Verses About Strength – 25 Encouraging Scripture Quotes,* http://www.whatchristianswanttoknow.com/bible-verses-about-strength-25-encouraging-scripture-quotes/

Josh, *22 Inspirational Bible Verses: Christian Quotes,* http://www.whatchristianswanttoknow.com/22-inspirational-bible-verses/

Want to Find Your Life Path? http://www.manifestyourpotential.com/self_discovery/1_identify_lifepath/topic_identify_life_path.htm

Burton, Valorie, *Five Keys to Realizing Your Potential,* http://www.cbn.com/finance/burton_potential.aspx

Horwath, Rich, *To Realize Your Potential, Dare to Be Different,* http://www.cnn.com/2012/02/24/opinion/horwath-strategy-different/index.html

Halstead, Rebecca, *Live by Example,* http://www.selfgrowth.com/articles/Live_By_Example.html

21 Ways to Be Inspired, http://www.beliefnet.com/Inspiration/2009/09/21-Ways-to-Be-Inspired.aspx?b=1&p=8

10 Simple Rules for a Happy Life, http://www.livingggood.com/inspiration/this-is-your-life/

How to Be Happy, http://rulestobehappy.tumblr.com/

Chapter 10

Quotes About Personal Growth, http://www.goodreads.com/quotes/tag/personal-growth

Gentry, Mike, *Seven Habits of Highly Effective Christians: Habit #1,* http://suite101.com/article/7-habits-of-highly-effective-christians-habit-1-a335664

Giving Up, 30 Bible Verses About, http://www.openbible.info/topics/giving_up

Esty, Chris, *25 Encouraging Bible Verses*, http://www.thebiblepost.com/encouraging-bible-verses

Top 10 Reasons Why Losers Give Up: And How Not to Be a Loser Too!, http://www.arvinddevalia.com/blog/2012/06/07/how-not-to-be-a-loser/

22 Reasons to Never Give Up, http://www.pickthebrain.com/blog/22-reasons-to-never-give-up/

The Positive Approach, http://www.trans4mind.com/positive/

How to Solve Any Problem, http://www.usereffect.com/topic/how-to-solve-any-problem

Edberg, Henrik, *How to Solve a Problem: 6 Quick and Powerful Tips*, http://www.positivityblog.com/index.php/2009/07/10/how-to-solve-a-problem-6-quick-and-powerful-tips/

How to Make Dreams Come True, http://thinksimplenow.com/happiness/my-dreams-come-true/

About the Author

Zenovia Andrews is a highly sought after speaker, author, life coach, and business development strategist. She is the Founder and CEO of Max Out, Inc., a successful company committed to empowering and revitalizing women to discover their purpose and walk in their divine destiny in life while radically "Maxing Out" their unparalleled potential regardless of the obstacles or challenges in their way.

She works alongside her loving husband, Senior Pastor Anthony Andrews II, as a Co-Founder of Kingdom Agenda International Ministry, Panama City, FL. Zenovia is also a Co-Founder of Fresh Aura, Inc., a very prominent company that equips and enlightens women of all nationalities to embrace the classy chic and fabulous that's within them by discovering the couture in the everyday.

Zenovia has over 12 years of extensive and cross-functional expertise in corporate training, performance management, business development and sales consulting, and team building from several international corporations; to name a few: Pfizer Inc., Novartis Pharmaceuticals, Rubicon Healthcare Consultants, Fresh Aura, Inc., and Kingdom Agenda International Ministry.

Zenovia is the epitome of what MaxOut stands for. She has spent the last 15 years helping countless women overcome the challenges of negative thinking to transform their lives with a healthy new mindset. Being abandoned as a child at the age of six months and growing up around drugs and alcohol, Zenovia knows first-hand how the mind and emotions can affect your whole outlook on life.

www.ingramcontent.com/pod-product-compliance
Lightning Source LLC
Chambersburg PA
CBHW071120090426
42736CB00012B/1966